D0221128

Rituals, Ceremonies, and Cultural Meaning in Higher Education

Critical Studies in Education and Culture Series

Rituals, Ceremonies, and Cultural Meaning in Higher Education

Kathleen Manning

Critical Studies in Education and Culture Series
Edited by Henry A. Giroux

Bergin & Garvey
Westport, Connecticut • London

Library of Congress Cataloging-in-Publication Data

Manning, Kathleen, 1954–
 Rituals, ceremonies, and cultural meaning in higher education / by Kathleen Manning.
  p. cm.—(Critical studies in education and culture series, ISSN 1064–8615)
 Includes bibliographical references (p.) and index.
 ISBN 0–89789–504–5 (alk. paper)
 1. Education, Higher—Social aspects—United States. 2. Educational
anthropology—United States. I. Title. II. Series.
LC191.9.M26 2000
306.43—dc21   99–055887

British Library Cataloguing in Publication Data is available.

Copyright © 2000 by Kathleen Manning

All rights reserved. No portion of this book may be
reproduced, by any process or technique, without the
express written consent of the publisher.

Library of Congress Catalog Card Number: 99–055887
ISBN: 0–89789–504–5
ISSN: 1064–8615

First published in 2000

Bergin & Garvey, 88 Post Road West, Westport, CT 06881
An imprint of Greenwood Publishing Group, Inc.
www.greenwood.com

Printed in the United States of America

The paper used in this book complies with the
Permanent Paper Standard issued by the National
Information Standards Organization (Z39.48–1984).

10 9 8 7 6 5 4 3 2 1

Contents

Series Foreword

Educational reform has fallen upon hard times. The traditional assumption that schooling is fundamentally tied to the imperatives of citizenship designed to educate students to exercise civic leadership and public service has been eroded. The schools are now the key institution for producing professional, technically trained, credentialized workers for whom the demands of citizenship are subordinated to the vicissitudes of the marketplace and the commercial public sphere. Given the current corporate and right wing assault on public and higher education, coupled with the emergence of a moral and political climate that has shifted to a new social Darwinism, the issues that framed the democratic meaning, purpose, and use to which education might aspire have been displaced by more vocational and narrowly ideological considerations.

The war waged against the possibilities of an education wedded to the precepts of a real democracy is not merely ideological. Against the backdrop of reduced funding for public schooling, the call for privatization, vouchers, cultural uniformity, and choice, there are the often ignored larger social realities of material power and oppression. On the national level, there has been a vast resurgence of racism. This is evident in the passing of anti-immigration laws such as proposition 187 in California, the dismantling of the welfare state, the demonization of black youth that is taking place in the popular media, and the remarkable attention provided by the media to forms of race talk that argue for the intellectual inferiority of blacks or dismiss calls for racial justice as simply a holdover from the "morally bankrupt" legacy of the 1960s.

Poverty is on the rise among children in the United States, with 20 percent of all children under the age of eighteen living below the poverty line. Unemployment is growing at an alarming rate for poor youth of color, especially in the urban centers. While black youth are policed and disciplined in and out of the nation's schools, conservative and liberal educators define education through the ethnically limp discourses of privatization, national standards, and global competitiveness.

Many writers in the critical education tradition have attempted to challenge the right wing fundamentalism behind educational and social reform in both the United States and abroad while simultaneously providing ethical signposts for a public discourse about education and democracy that is both prophetic and transformative. Eschewing traditional categories, a diverse number of critical theorists and educators have successfully exposed the political and ethical implications of the cynicism and despair that have become endemic to the discourse of schooling and civic life. In its place, such educators strive to provide a language of hope that inextricably links the struggle over schooling to understanding and transforming our present social and cultural dangers.

At the risk of overgeneralizing, both cultural studies theorists and critical educators have emphasized the importance of understanding theory as the grounded basis for "intervening into contexts and power . . . in order to enable people to act more strategically in ways that may change their context for the better" (Grossberg, 1996, p. 143). Moreover, theorists in both fields have argued for the primacy of the political by calling for and struggling to produce critical public spaces, regardless of how fleeting they may be, in which "popular cultural resistance is explored as a form of political resistance" (Bailey & Hall, 1992, p. 19). Such writers have analyzed the challenges that teachers will have to face in defining a new mission for education, one that is linked to honoring the experiences, concerns, and diverse histories and languages that give expression to the multiple narratives that engage and challenge the legacy of democracy.

Equally significant is the insight of recent critical educational work that connects the politics of difference with concrete strategies for addressing the crucial relationships between schooling and the economy, and citizenship and the politics of meaning in communities of multicultural, multiracial, and multilingual schools.

Critical Studies in Education and Culture attempts to address and demonstrate how scholars working in the fields of cultural studies and the critical pedagogy might join together in a radical project and practice informed by theoretically rigorous discourses that affirm the critical but refuse the cynical, and establish hope as central to a critical pedagogical and political practice but eschew a romantic utopianism. Central to such a project is the issue of how pedagogy might provide cultural studies theorists and educators with an opportunity to engage pedagogical practices that are not only transdisciplinary, transgressive, and oppositional, but also connected to a wider project designed to further racial, economic, and political democracy[1] (Zavarzadeh & Morton, 1992, p. 10). By taking seriously the relations between culture and power, we further the possibilities of resistance, struggle, and change.

Critical Studies in Education and Culture is committed to publishing work that opens a narrative space that affirms the contextual and the specific while simultaneously recognizing the ways in which such spaces are shot through with issues of power. The series attempts to continue an important legacy of theoretical work in cultural studies in which related debates on pedagogy are understood and addressed within the larger context of social responsibility, civic courage, and the reconstruction of democratic public life. We must keep in mind Raymond Williams's insight that the "deepest impulse (informing cultural politics) is the desire to make learning part of the process of social change itself" (1989, p. 158). Education as a cultural pedagogical practice takes place across multiple sites, which include not only schools and universities but also the mass media, popular culture, and other public spheres, and signals how within diverse contexts, education makes us both subjects of and subject to relations of power.

This series challenges the current return to the primacy of market values and simultaneous retreat from politics so evident in the recent work of educational theorists, legislators, and policy analysts. Professional relegitimation in a troubled time seems to be the order of the day as an increasing number of academics both refuse to recognize public and higher education as critical public spheres and offer little or no resistance to the ongoing vocationalization of schooling, the continuing evisceration of the intellectual labor force, and the current assaults on the working poor, the elderly, and women and children.[2]

Emphasizing the centrality of politics, culture, and power, *Critical Studies in Education and Culture* will deal with pedagogical issues that contribute in imaginative and transformative ways to our understanding of how critical knowledge, democratic values, and social practices can provide a basis for teachers, students, and other cultural workers to redefine their role as engaged and public intellectuals. Each volume will attempt to rethink the relationship between language and experience, pedagogy and human agency, and ethics and social responsibility as part of a larger project for engaging and deepening the prospects of democratic schooling in a multiracial and multicultural society. *Critical Studies in Education and Culture* takes on the responsibility of witnessing and addressing the most pressing problems of public schooling and civic life, and engages culture as a crucial site and strategic force for productive social change.

Henry A. Giroux

REFERENCES

Bailey, D., & Hall, S. (1992). The vertigo of displacement. *Ten 8, 2*(3), p. 19.

Grossberg, L. (1996). Toward a genealogy of the state of cultural studies. In C. Nelson & D.P. Gaonkar (Eds.). *Disciplinarity and dissent in cultural studies.* New York: Routledge.

Williams, R. (1989). *What I Came to Say.* London: Hutchinson-Radius.

Zavarzadeh, M., & Morton, D. (1992). Theory, Pedagogy, Politics: The crisis of the "subject" in the humanities. In. M. Zavarzadeh & D. Morton (Eds.). *Theory, Pedagogy, Politics: Texts for change.* Urbana, IL: University of Illinois Press.

NOTES

1. At issue here is neither ignoring the boundaries of discipline-based knowledge nor simply fusing different disciplines, but creating theoretical paradigms, questions, and knowledge that cannot be taken up within the policed boundaries of the existing disciplines.

2. The term "professional legitimation" comes from a personal correspondence with Professor Jeff Williams of East Carolina University.

Acknowledgments

When I began my long journey exploring rituals and ceremonies in higher education, I was hosted and welcomed into a remarkable community of women. Sheila Murphy, then Dean of Students at Mount Holyoke College, invited me to conduct research on that campus. The Mount Holyoke students, alumnae, and administrators who served as respondents, friends, and colleagues taught me a great deal about excellence and achievement.

In 1989, I was welcomed into a community of substantial excellence and quality at the University of Vermont. The students and faculty within the Higher Education and Student Affairs graduate program have been a source of inspiration and support for eleven years. I particularly want to thank "HESA family" member, Amiko Matsumoto, who skillfully and generously proofread the final copy of *Rituals, Ceremonies, and Cultural Performances in Higher Education*.

Marc vanderHeyden, Jenni Cernosia, and other administrators at Saint Michael's College generously allowed me to enter their community to conduct research. Only through the warmth and kindness of my higher education colleagues was this book conceived, written, and published.

Finally, thank you to George Kuh who continues to offer me his support whenever possible.

Chapter 1

The Rituals of Higher Education

Culture is a blank space, a highly respected, empty pigeonhole. Economists call it "tastes" and leave it severely alone. Most philosophers ignore it—to their own loss. Marxists treat it obliquely as ideology or superstructure. Psychologists ignore it, by concentrating on child subjects. Historians bend it any way they like (Douglas, 1982, p. 183).

Reflexive artifacts, magic, priestly intermediaries, group crisis, ceremonial patterns, liminal interstices, comic levity, sacred seriousness (Raybin, 1990; Turner, F., 1990). These terms, washed in meaning, are a slice of the abundant anthropological literature about rituals. As these terms imply, there is something magical and mystical about rituals. Even, or perhaps especially, in postmodern societies, rituals bind us in the most primordial levels through community and culture-building, individual and communal celebration.

Interestingly enough, with all of its attention to the life of the mind (often separated from culture-building endeavors), higher education is awash with ritual activity. The academic year is bookended with convocation and commencement. In between is a long line of building dedications, class galas, tree-planting ceremonies, alumni merrymaking, and founder's commemorations. Clearly, rituals and ceremonies are cultural markers of college campuses.

ANTHROPOLOGICAL PERSPECTIVES

Campus rituals, traditions, sagas, myths, artifacts, and ceremonies have been researched in an attempt to expand our understanding of faculty, students, and administrators (Clark, 1972; Kuh, Schuh, Whitt, & Associates, 1991; Kuh & Whitt, 1988; Leemon, 1972; Manning, 1989a, 1989b, 1993, 1994a, 1994b; Manning & Eaton, 1993; Tierney, 1988). As a means of making sense of college cultural events, higher education theorists and researchers rely on anthropological literature as a theoretical base. These authors make meaning of the everyday experiences of campus inhabitants using anthropological ideas about culture as a guide. Anthropologists study human nature, particularly the creative transformation of human existence. In other words, at interest is how people build, learn, and transform culture in ways that create meaning and give definition to their existence.

Seeing the Extraordinary in the Ordinary

Rituals are more than "social glue" that holds society together (DeFlem, 1991). They happen too often to serve only that function; their spiritual, religious, and emotional nature point to something more. Despite the commonplace presence of rituals and ceremonies on college campuses, there is nothing ordinary about these activities. Rituals, with their fluid, dynamic, complex, and adaptable form, are a potent ingredient of campus cultural demarcation and transformation. In ways explored in this book, rituals maintain while simultaneously transform campus cultures. This dual quality of rituals, cultural conservation and transformation, can be used to explain some of the most interesting aspects of human culture and meaning making.

Interpretive Anthropology and Underlying Tenets

This book, borrowing from interpretive anthropology (Geertz, 1973; 1983; 1988) spotlights the following tenets: (a) Culture is revealed and forms of life are expressed through the actions and words of community members. (b) Human communities are dynamic, complex, and everchanging environments revealed through analysis of cultural events. (c) Commonplace rituals and ceremonies play a central role in the cultural work of human meaning making.

Communal and Individual Histories. Interpretive anthropology embodies the assumption that "culture mediates all human behavior" (Ortner, 1984, p. 132). Presented in a tapestry of patterns, culture is always present in the ways it creates a backdrop against which individual behavior, accounts of past practices, and community expectations of members' actions are performed and judged. From the interpretive anthropology perspective participants' behavior can be viewed in the context of the past, present, and future of the individual and community. As such, rituals and other cultural forms serve as a "spiritual glue"—a means to keep humanity from coming apart at the seams (McLaren, 1986, p. 189). Rituals, in conjunction with other cultural observances, hold the nothingness of reality and culture together.

For the purposes of this book I assume that ritual behaviors and beliefs are neither predetermined nor created anew but, rather, fashioned on cultural forms inherited from the past. "It is an act without a source, an origin or an 'author'" (Morgan, 1984, p. 82). The cultural messages embodied in rituals and ceremonies are dramatized, explicated, and symbolized throughout a college campus.

Dynamic, Complex, and Everchanging. The interpretive anthropological perspective assumes that human beings, through agency and free choice, continually make and remake their existence (Giddens, 1979, 1982, 1993). This is possible because while culture provides the script for rituals, ceremonies, and other culture-building activities, humans are free to change that script as they see fit. The result is complexity, confusion, and dynamism that allow for cultural change and transformation. Building on the old adage that you cannot step into the same river twice, you cannot experience the same ritual or ceremony twice. While they are hauntingly similar, they are paradoxically distinct.

Meaning-Making Human Activity. A foundational concern in interpretative anthropology is current, as opposed to historical, meaning as interpreted by culture participants. While a historical tracing of individual rituals and ceremonies is surely a valuable research project, the interpretive perspective used for the research in this book focused on the here and now meaning making of campus participants. I focused on discovering the idiosyncratic, personal meaning that college participants made of the rituals and ceremonies they attended—or in many instances, about which they heard stories. Rituals, from such a perspective, can be viewed as "a cultural 'agent', energetic, subversive, creative, socially critical" (Grimes, 1990, p. 144), a culture-building activity.

This interpretation and meaning-making activity is possible because there is a content expressed in ritual unspoken in ordinary circumstances (Raybin, 1990). Ritual "allows communication that cannot be stated in a clearer, more direct fashion" (Schwartzman, 1982, p. 15). Where else could one dramatize the rich history of the institution, encourage students to become all they are able, and urge young people to follow their most far-reaching aspirations?

This ability to communicate extraordinary meaning creates a medium to express the uncommon and remarkable dimensions of campus culture. The meaning conveyed and interpreted during these special times includes the common sense knowledge perceived by members of the community as well as their hopes and dreams of themselves and the college.

FOCUS OF THE RITUAL RESEARCH

The focus of this research was to explore campus culture as revealed through rituals and ceremonies. The focus on rituals and ceremonies as cultural forms was chosen for three reasons: (a) higher education is replete with ritualistic activities, (b) the well-established anthropological literature base serves as a fertile theoretical background, and (c) rituals are rich depositories of the accumulated meaning within a college culture. By examining the form of the rituals and ceremonies, the meanings of college culture could be understood.

The remaining sections of this chapter review the basic theoretical perspectives concerning rituals. This context provides the reader with knowledge about rituals, meaning, and anthropological understanding.

RITES OF PASSAGE, SECULAR CEREMONIES, AND CULTURAL PERFORMANCES

Among various choices three forms of rituals have been delineated in the anthropological literature: rites of passage (van Gennep, 1960), secular ceremony (Moore & Myerhoff, 1977), and cultural performances (MacAloon, 1984).

Rites of Passage

In 1908 Arnold van Gennep established the field of ritual study in anthropology by positing the definition of "rites of passage." Resting on the anthropological perspective of structuralism, he defined rituals as composed of a universal tri-part structure: separation, transition, and incorporation. While van Gennep's interest ran to non-Western activities such as fertility rites, protection and divination rites, and purification ceremonies, Western ritual participants can grasp his concepts by considering activities such as marriages, baptisms, and funerals. In Western societies, ritual "performance is usually optional, not prescribed" (Ashley, 1990, p. xx). His definition of rites of passage is further discussed in chapter 3.

Secular Ceremony

Sally Moore and Barbara Myerhoff (1977) added to the anthropological theory of rituals through their work concerning secular ceremonies. Rejecting the universal structure of rites of passage, these two theorists described rituals in dynamic and fluid terms. Secular ceremonies through dynamic action and culturally relevant themes could profoundly affect institutional structures. The properties they described as characterizing secular ceremonies are (a) repetition, (b) self-conscious action on the part of participants, (c) stylized or special behavior, (d) order, (e) an evocative presentational style, and (f) a collective dimension.

According to Moore and Myerhoff's explanation of secular ceremonies, these events shape, reinforce, and transform institutional structures. Because they are formed and re-formed with each performance, secular ceremonies restate what "is" while they foreshadow what "can be." They exist within both the "realm of possibility and make-believe" (Morgan, 1984, p. 79). They take socially constructed institutional structures (including beliefs and structural patterns) and simultaneously reinforce and transform those structures. These concepts are described in chapter 5.

Cultural Performances

John MacAloon (1984) used the term cultural performances to describe events that were less stylized than secular ceremonies and less formal than rites of passage. Cultural performances

> are more than entertainment, more than didactic or persuasive formulations, and more than cathartic indulgences. They are occasions in which as a culture or society we reflect upon and define ourselves with alternatives, and eventually change in some ways while remaining the same in others (p. 1).

Resembling rehearsals more than the formal performances of rituals or secular ceremonies, cultural performances include the community picnics, class talent shows, and football game gaiety of college life (see chapter 9).

The concepts of rites of passage, secular ceremony, and cultural performances serve as a framework to provide insight for the reader into campus culture events. To reduce confusion about terminology, the more generic term, rituals, is primarily used in this text.

TYPES OF RITUALS

In addition to the three areas of anthropological study described above, the following ritual types are described: reification, revitalization, resistance, incorporation, investiture, entrance and exit, and healing. These seven types of rituals are highlighted due to their prevalence or importance on college campuses. Additionally, several of these types (e.g., resistance) point to some integral campus culture issues.

Rituals of Reification

Rituals of reification assure participants that, particularly in the context of their present living or working environment, their choices are of value. In higher education where students make personal and financial sacrifices to attend college, ritualistic declarations about higher education's mission, the importance of a postsecondary degree, and the relevance of college culture assure them that these sacrifices are not made in vain. For example, the messages and actions of convocations at the start of their freshman year assure students of their elite standing, impending career success, and abiding status as members of the community. Students are assured and the culture takes root through the continual ritual action of the academic environment.

Rituals of Revitalization

A ritual of revitalization is a "processual event that functions to inject a renewal of commitment into the motivations and values of the ritual participants" (McLaren, 1986, p. 80). Through formal and informal forms, these rituals revitalize the college's founding values, restate and update underlying assumptions, and enlist new recruits into the belief structure of the institution. Examples of these rituals described through the case studies in this book include Presidential Inauguration, Mary Lyon's Birthday, and Charter Day.

Rituals of revitalization can take an informal structure in the form of meetings, rehearsals, and announcements. Meetings and practices are often held with the senior class prior to graduation. In addition to being a drill of what to expect during the commencement ceremony, these meetings set a tone, establish expectations, and, in the context of rehearsal, serve as another opportunity for the students to hear the founding beliefs, assumptions, and values. In other words, the actual ritual is not the only opportunity for meaning to be conveyed. Meaning-making opportunities precede the ritual, occur during its enactment, and linger after the event is complete.

Rituals of Resistance

The meaning-making activity of college rituals does not necessarily proceed in an orderly, uncontested manner. Students, in particular, often dispute the cultural meanings embodied in rituals. They can, at times, create their own rituals, separate from the administratively sanctioned rituals of campus life. In fact, for many students, these are the *real* rituals of campus life, a more accurate reflection of the true meaning of college living.

Rituals of resistance are "agonistic" ... they are rituals of conflict .... students are transformed into combatants and antagonists; hidden grudges and emotions are mobilized for the purpose of rupturing the culturally axiomatic rules of school and subverting the grammars of mainstream classroom discourse (McLaren, 1986, pp. 80-81).

Campus events that meet the definition of rituals of resistance are fraternity and sorority hazing, champagne-stimulated antics of commencement, and rites of spring observed on many campuses.

Rituals of Incorporation

This category of rituals delineates events that, often at the end of another ritual, welcome the person into a new community. Rituals of incorporation often involve "libations, ceremonial visiting . . . the sharing of bread and salt or a beverage, the sharing of a meal" (van Gennep, 1960, p. 24).

College campuses, particularly after rituals such as commencement when the student is crossing from one role (student) to a second role (alumni), ease the transition with a reception, food, and company. The student is not left after graduation to fend on his or her own, thrown out of the community with no ceremonial bridge. Instead, the transition to alumni and college graduate is facilitated with refreshments, final farewells, and fellowship. Postgraduation receptions often contain festive elements of the just-completed ritual as students wear their academic regalia, carry flowers bestowed upon them by family and friends, and enjoy the presence of major graduation actors (university administrators, commencement speakers).

Rituals of Investiture

Presidential inaugurations and the accompanying festivities of such events are the primary higher education examples of this type of ritual. While past practice relegated this ritual type to kings, queens, and emperors, higher education has reserved these rituals only for presidents. The chair of the board of trustees, ostensibly the highest ranking hierarchical role on campus, is not granted the pomp and circumstance of presidential inaugurations.

As with all rituals, presidential inaugurations endow the office of the president with meaning beyond the bureaucratic or administrative tasks of the office. Inaugurations are one of the most public ceremonies held on college campuses. They symbolize the strength of the institution as exemplified by the prominence of the ceremony and the leadership of the president.

During inauguration the president is vested with the power and authority of the office. Visiting dignitaries from local and far-flung colleges and universities attend the ceremony in a gesture that welcomes the newly inducted president into the ranks of higher education's elite. Medieval regalia is augmented with presidential seals, medallions, and a mace. Each symbol of the presidential office is dutifully described in the inauguration program. The fact that the arrival of a new college president is relatively infrequent endows inauguration ceremonies with even more meaning.

Rituals of Entering and Exiting

The act of crossing a threshold, whether in marriage, entering a new house, or embarking on a new stage of life, has traditionally been endowed with considerable meaning. Jews touch a mezuzah ("a casket attached to the doorpost which contains a piece of paper or ribbon upon which is written . . . the name of God") (van Gennep, 1960, p. 24); main doors frequently face a favored direction; guests are honored by being let in and out of the front door, used for such special occasions.

Colleges are not exempt from the sacrosanct nature of entrances and exits. The main approach to many campuses can be regally adorned with a gate or portal. Indiana University's gate and brick walk at its main entrance were built with funds donated by an alumni. Some on campus at the time argued that the construction of a formal entrance gate was "unnecessary" during demanding financial times when other more worthy projects went unfunded. Despite the protests, the gate was constructed with fine Indiana limestone. The main entrance to the campus, previously unobtrusively facing a main thoroughfare, was judged unworthy of a great university's main entrance.

Mount Holyoke College students used the terms "inside" and "outside" of the college's gates as a metaphor for their college careers and the developmental processes they experienced as students. Especially during commencement week activities, alumnae parade, and alumnae induction ceremonies, "inside the gates" was a place of sanctuary, retreat, and, of course, challenge. "Outside the gates" referred to the "real world" of jobs and postcollege responsibilities (Manning, 1989a).

Rituals of Healing

All college campuses, similar to families and communities, experience tragedy and crisis. Rituals of healing, whether consisting of funeral rites, memorial services, or tree plantings, are meant to help the survivors cope with the pain of loss. An untimely student death is marked with a memorial service open to all members of the college community. In the aftermath of a student protest, people gather to debrief and make sense of what occurred. Colleges across the country honor the victims of German concentration camps on Holocaust Remembrance Day. People protesting and trying to understand the Persian Gulf War gathered at community meetings, teach-ins, and vigils.

When a community does not partake of the healing qualities of healing rituals, the pain lingers longer than it should and interferes with community members' ability to return to their regular routine.

Additional Ritual Types

Due to the vast number of ritual types and the limited space in this book, Table 1 briefly summarizes a number of categories of rituals and ceremonies. The reader should note that some of these ritual types are rarely, if ever, enacted on college campuses.

Table 1

Types of Rituals

Anthropological theory	Within higher education
admission and entering	Orientation; Residence hall welcomes
adopting strangers	Honorary degree ceremonies
consecration	Centennial celebrations
death	Memorial services
exit	Retirement receptions
festivals	Community picnics
founding	Founder's Day observances
frontier crossing	Commencements
healing rites	Community meetings after a crisis
incorporation	Orientation picnics
initiation	Convocations*
intensity	Alumni gatherings; Alumnae Parade and Laurel Chain*
inversion	Student performances; Junior Show*
investiture	President inaugurations*
naming	Building dedications
pilgrimage	Homecomings
pledges	Honor society initiations
purification	Benedictions
rebellion	Spring Break vacations
resistance	Greek hazings
separation	Senior Week activities
songs	Alma maters

Compiled from McLaren (1986); Moore and Myerhoff (1977); V. Turner (1974), Turner and Turner (1985) and van Gennep (1960).

*Depicted in case studies within this book.

SIGNIFICANT THEMES IN COLLEGE RITUALS

Throughout the text of this book, descriptions of higher education rituals are offered and their attendant themes explored. As a preview to this discussion, several of these themes contained throughout this book are explained in this chapter: (a) mirroring the college's values, (b) punctuation and mediation of campus life, (c) power, and (d) criticism and parody.

Mirroring the College's Values

Rituals are events rich with messages, meanings, and statements about the college in which they are enacted. Among other functions, rituals express the traditions of a community, welcome and initiate new members, create a bridge between the here-and-now and the there-and-then, preview the passage from college living to outside college reality, express the community's beliefs and values, and celebrate members' accomplishments (Gardner, 1986; Gardner & Van der Veer, 1998; Turner, V. 1969; van Gennep, 1960).

Punctuation and Mediation of Campus Life

Social life as a collection of actions performed by individuals is bound by a set of rule governing behavior. Prospective students scrutinize college catalogues and admission viewbooks to assess community values, form expectations, and learn how they are to act. Any college administrator or faculty member who has participated in orientation knows that students hunger for knowledge about the community and clues about how they are to act in their newly adopted home.

Power

"Ritualization is a play of power" (Oosten, 1993, p. 107). Power, as expressed in ritual acts, is particularly effective when indirect claims to power are made (if the power invoked during ritual is attributed to a creator or spiritual being).

At Mount Holyoke College, the claims for power came from the myths and stories told about the founder, Mary Lyon. Myths and stories abound about the hardships she undertook (e.g., collecting pennies from area country women to found the institution) and serve as a foundation upon which ritual power, and subsequent personal power attributed to Mary Lyon, have been built. This was particularly illustrated by the rituals such as Founder's Day and the Laurel Chain, which were conducted at her grave, centrally located on campus.

Ritual power is an idea to be approached cautiously. The power traditionally discussed in ritual theories is hierarchical and patriarchal. Critical theorists (hooks, 1994; McLaren, 1986; Tierney, 1988) detail and challenge the patriarchal relationships advanced through cultural artifacts such as rituals. Given the fact that one of the research sites upon which this book is based is a women's college, these patriarchal themes may not only lack relevance but deserve close examination. While this women's college was certainly defined, at least in part, by the patriarchal themes defining all Western institutions, patriarchy in its rawest form was less evident in this environment than in coeducational institutions. Therefore, a different form of power should be considered for the rituals described from these less patriarchal settings.

Criticism and Parody

A theme often present in rituals is criticism and parody. Using comedy, farce, and cultural faux pas, rituals have the capability to create situations where community members laugh at themselves, make fun of each other, and treat the most serious issues in a manner that pokes fun and creates absurdity. This capacity of rituals to criticize and juxtapose the serious with the lighthearted encourages participants to look at these critical issues in a different light. As such, a well-worn, accepted belief may undergo a long needed reexamination when seen from a lighter side. Rituals can be "performances through which a society may look at itself, reaffirm its values, or criticize its practices" (Morgan, 1984, p. 79).

PURPOSE OF THE BOOK

The primary purpose of this book is to elicit a conversation about rituals. I seek to link the cultural action of rituals to larger meanings created in higher education and college life. The multiple voices expressed in the conversation created through this book emanate from the research respondents, anthropologists, higher education theorists, and myself.

This book about campus rituals is a blend of anthropological and higher education theory. Although similar to the subdiscipline of anthropology and education (Spindler, 1987), higher education is rarely a field of study within anthropology. Not only do I rely on the assumptions of the subdiscipline of anthropology and education (culture as socially constructed, assumptions and beliefs as underpinning guides for behavior, etc.), I seek to augment this subdiscipline.

This book explicates the unique culture of higher education through the medium of the rituals and ceremonies. At issue are how college members interpret and give these rituals meaning, why they have such an enduring quality, and how they relate to a campus community. These questions are explored in the context of findings gleaned from qualitative research, including respondent interviews, ritual observations, and document analysis. The creation, communication, and perpetuation of higher education culture—its traditions, ideals, and beliefs—are the focal point of the discussion.

A secondary purpose of *Rituals, Ceremonies, and Cultural Meaning in Higher Education* is to illustrate how members of college communities express meaning through activities such as convocations, celebrations, and graduations. These events mark significant events in the life of a college and community. The meaning created around these events persists in the memory of alumni, colors the nature of college community for undergraduate students, and provides a vehicle to express the founding beliefs and values of the institution.

An important contribution of this research is the expression that rituals enacted on college campuses are the fabric out of which community is formed. Without overstating their importance, one must recognize that the people who make up college communities create rituals and ceremonies in an attempt to give meaning to their lives. The anthropological literature of rituals firmly rests on this idea that meaning is the raison d'etre of rituals and ceremonies. Through these events, community members find connections to others, link themselves with a world greater than themselves, bind their individual histories to community ones and vice versa, and openly and evocatively express their emotions.

Objectives and Questions

Questions addressed in this book include the following: (a) Why do colleges persist with rituals and ceremonies in ways that other contemporary institutions do not? (b) What meaning do individual community members derive from the rituals? (c) How do rituals evolve, endure, and re-create themselves? and (d) What is it about human nature that drives us to become emotionally linked to these events which package so much content and meaning?

The qualitative research upon which this book is based used the following questions to guide the data collection and analysis: (a) What role do rituals play as students, administrators, and faculty make sense of the college? (b) What occurs during these rituals? (c) What overt and covert meanings are conveyed during the rituals? (d) What interpretations are made by ritual participants? (e) What messages and meaning about their colleges are interpreted by students, alumni, and administrators from these events? (f) Did rituals perpetuate the traditional purpose, goals, and values of a college?

Caveats

Many people debate whether all campuses, particularly community colleges or recently established institutions, have rituals. Does a college have to be old with a rich history for the events to be rituals? What can administrators and students do to perpetuate rituals that build community spirit? How do they know that they performed the rituals correctly? Why do these events continue—even after their usefulness appears to be finished? And, my favorite question: can an institution start "new" rituals?

The term "new rituals," possibly an oxymoron, provides insight into our thinking about rituals. Rituals surround us every day. Where a student parks her car, how someone registers for class, how one waits on dining hall lines, the method with which students parade to class are all examples of rituals in the Goffman tradition of habits (1959). While they are interesting in their own right, this book does not discuss the ritualized habits and actions of everyday life. Rather, it is the administratively sponsored, public rituals that are of interest here. The rituals analyzed and discussed are the community-wide events that create opportunities to name college beliefs, restate history, create and perpetuate values, and heal the community in a crisis. While I believe that all campuses have rituals (those events that form, state, and perpetuate the character of the community), the rituals discussed in this book are based on long-standing traditions deeply embedded in higher education culture. These rituals include convocations, baccalaureate ceremonies, graduations, founder's days, and presidential inaugurations. I would not argue that less formal occurrences such as registration procedures, student habits, and family weekends are not rituals, but the description and analysis of those events is left to another author.

PREVIEW OF RITUAL CASES

The methodology underlying this book is constructivist inquiry (Guba & Lincoln, 1989; Lincoln & Guba, 1985). This educational qualitative research methodology was used to observe rituals in a variety of locations over a period of ten years. The research products are case studies embedded between theoretical chapters. These cases illustrate the rituals and convey the meaning embedded in and interpreted by the people participating in those events. While one cannot entirely understand or experience the rituals through these cases, they are written so that the reader can vicariously know them. Through this understanding, readers can enrich the rituals currently enacted on their campuses, create "new" rituals, and enhance their and others' understanding of the rituals and ceremonies in which they participate.

SUMMARY

The qualitative research used to collect data on the rituals, secular ceremonies, and cultural performances summarized in the case studies of this book was conducted on four campuses over a period of ten years. The time and place of both the research and the interpretation is important as one must place rituals in their sociohistoric context (Flanigan, 1990). In light of the context in which they were enacted, the following questions can be asked in regard to the interpretations offered by respondents: (a) What were the national higher education issues that were defining individual college culture? (b) How do the history and long-term themes of an individual campus define the individual rituals and cultural events? (c) How do people define themselves locally in the context of events that occur globally? Therefore, the interpretations offered are situated in twentieth-century United States culture.

Chapter 2

Presidential Inauguration

If we do it right, we will be like the archangels.

—President Marc vanderHeyden

MARKING THE OCCASION

Whether labeled an inauguration, investiture, or installation, the ceremony celebrating a new college president is a joyous occasion. Elaborate invitations and inauguration announcements herald an occasion of great joy for a campus.

The inauguration of Marc vanderHeyden at Saint Michael's College in Colchester, Vermont, was truly an occasion to acclaim. One step onto the campus convinced any visitor that the ceremony, to be held in the athletic complex, was a community observance. Fanfare and jubilation were introduced by school-color-coordinated balloons flying from every lamppost along the college walkways. The purple and gold balloons, the appearance of off-campus visitors, and the academics clothed in full regalia were signs that something out of the ordinary was about to occur.

The presence of sports equipment in the athletic complex confirmed the fact that the newly assigned ceremonial space was primarily used for basketball games. But on this day, the large hall was irrefutably transformed from those utilitarian purposes. To achieve this metamorphosis, the audience would have to ignore the obvious—basketball hoops, bleachers, transient folding chairs, and floor-shielding blue tarpaulin. Nothing, not even the somewhat inadequate public address system, echoing off the bleachers, wooden floor, and high ceiling, could dampen the hope built into this occasion. This hope was present regardless of the fact that with presidential turnover relatively high in colleges and universities, new leadership is more common than in the past.

The distinctive quality of the occasion was further suggested by long, colorful banners hanging behind the stage. Taken from their usual perch in the college chapel, the banners sported likenesses of St. Edmund, patron saint of the college's founding order of Catholic priests, and Saint Michael the Archangel, namesake of the institution. The latter's likeness was gaunt and sunken-cheeked, reflecting the seriousness of his task to slay the dragon at his feet. The banners of the saints contrasted with the athletic conference banners hanging on the opposite side of the gym. The four hundred plus spectators attending the inauguration had exchanged their customary jeans and informal dress for slacks, dresses, and starched shirts. Given the Vermont and campus norm of informality, this proper dress further marked the occasion as exceptional.

Ceremonies, including inaugurations, present occasions to evoke meaning through music, to celebrate community members, and to add a touch of spirituality. The impending ceremony would entail a mere two hours of the life of the man being installed to the campus's highest office. Though it would occupy a relatively insignificant amount of time, its ceremonial embellishments such as speeches, symbols, and dress would create the illusion of extended time; changing the sense of space and time, endowing the occasion with significance.

To further punctuate the formality and importance of the presidential inauguration, certain procedures had been followed. The platform party was painstakingly composed of board of trustee members, emeriti presidents, faculty representatives, student delegates, alumni notables, and staff and administrative leadership. Logistics were meticulously planned from the processional to the recessional. An address by the newly installed president would delineate the hopes and dreams of the new leadership. Music would punctuate the performance. College choruses, university bands, and student musicians added spirit. Whether it's the traditional "Pomp and Circumstance" or a commissioned selection, music is essential to an academic ceremony.

Bagpipers dressed in green blazers and matching kilts stood on the arts center steps piping as spectators arrived on campus. The five young bagpipers possessed an obvious joy in performing. They led the academic procession of board of trustees members, specially invited delegates, students, platform party, and regalia-clad faculty and administrators into the athletic complex. Their music awakened the audience to the fact that the ceremony was beginning.

THE CEREMONY

Procession

Faculty marshals led the inauguration procession into the athletic complex. At the head of the procession were international students carrying flags from their home countries. Dressed in their traditional, non-Western clothing, these students represented the distant boundaries of the college. Assorted colors graced the stage as students placed their flags in stanchions. These students and the countries they represented were notable to this community and would, of course, be included in the ceremony. Their prominence at the head of the procession and their place of honor on the stage further reinforced the idea that this was not a provincial institution.

Inaugurations, paradoxically a quintessential internal event, create an opportunity to transcend local boundaries. During inaugurations, colleges can simultaneously celebrate their missions, purposes, and histories while acknowledging their place in the world community. Few, if any, college celebrations extend the institution's boundaries in such a manner.

Regalia

Blue, brown, gold, red, and green gowns mixed with the traditionally austere black ones at the inauguration. Any academic ceremony would be incomplete without medieval-originated regalia and the constant confusion about its origin and meaning. Thankfully, inauguration programs often summarize the meaning of the regalia, which was introduced to American institutions in the mid-1800s. While the black robes matched the reserved character of academic professions, alternative colors asserted the autonomy of various higher education institutions. Hoods representing degrees and institutions emitted a burst of colors: blue for education, maize for agriculture, green for medicine, apricot for nursing, copper for economics, yellow for science, scarlet for theology. The discipline-associated color on the hood was accompanied, often with little regard for pleasing color combinations, by the degree-granting institution's colors: purple and gold for Saint Michael's, green and gold for neighboring University of Vermont, among others.

Talent and research capability differences are essentially erased when faculty don their regalia, march in an academic procession, and convene in a setting where academic rank becomes invisible. Faculty members all appear scholarly when dressed in their academic robes.

African American students, faculty, and administrators recast academic tradition with the addition of African kente cloth. Chevrons, hoods, and trim were adapted in a marvelous display of yellow. The poetic license taken with the ancient form added a new, though paradoxically old, statement to the faculty members' and administrators' academic identity.

One would not think that something as innocuous as color could have such a powerful effect on the tone and tenor of a ceremony. Class, school, and discipline colors were used to situate the celebration in a time and place. The color worn represented the group to which one belonged, the community of which one was a part. Color, in this way, was a metaphor for affiliation, connection, and unity.

Delegates

Delegates selected to represent their college or university donned their regalia, joined the processional, and welcomed the new president into the higher education community. A large number of delegates from as many institutions as possible meant that the president belonged to an influential cohort. Greetings and congratulations from nearby and far-flung institutions were proudly displayed in the cases lining the athletic center walls.

A delegate's institutional affiliation and that college's founding date were highlighted in a separate chronological listing in the inauguration program. The precious space devoted to the delegate and institutional listing betrayed the race to record as many institutions as possible. Harvard University began the list with its 1636 founding date; the list concluded with Showa Boston Institution for Language and Culture, founded in 1988. The date, accompanying a delegate's or speaker's name, placed that person within the legacy of higher education. The date and institution established an association with a cohort, a history, and a belief structure.

Colleges and universities were not the only institutions represented that day. Higher education delegates were joined by representatives from the state, federal, and local governments. The Vermont lieutenant governor, an alumnus state senator, and a former governor joined faculty, staff, students, administrators, alumni, and international partners. The religious affiliation of the institution was demonstrated by the presence of the diocese bishop, Society of St. Edmund representatives, and a celebrated local rabbi.

Opening and Greetings

The master of ceremonies used the loosely translated Latin welcome about "enthusiastic support" as a way to introduce the "eating and drinking" that were to commence after the ceremony. Following this welcome to all present, each campus constituency took the opportunity to offer his or her individualized welcome. A college is composed of different constituencies with vastly disparate needs and perspectives. While each group often believes its perspective should predominate, the president's job is to tactfully and artfully juggle those disparate perspectives. Representatives of those constituencies offered greetings to the new president in turn, welcomed him into the local campus community and community at large. As such, a litany of greetings was unleashed on the president and spectators.

Representing the faculty, a political science professor referred to their role of nurturing "the intellect informed by the heart." His prominence as the first speaker among the others established the foremost place of faculty within this academic institution.

A student from the Class of 2000, a milestone for any small liberal arts institution, employed a metaphor of buying a car to express her confidence that she had picked the right college. The audience responded to her creativity, poise, and articulate manner with rapt attention and enthusiastic applause. Though students were only sparsely represented in the audience, they were prominently featured in the inauguration's proceedings.

The staff representative reminded the audience and the new president that "this college prides itself as being a supportive community." Greeters used their short time in the spotlight to inform the new president of significant issues within their constituency. The staff representative recounted, with some surprise, a story of how the new president had won over that group by going from office to office when he first arrived on campus, showing up at 11:00 p.m. when only the custodial staff was present, and had become a "regular in the student dining hall." Those gestures acknowledged the unsung staff heroes of the college, the backbone of this small community. The president knew that this group kept the institution running, nurtured the students, and provided continuity. Unable to find complete satisfaction in their meager salaries, staff members were dependent on occasional words of thanks and gestures of gratitude for their rewards. The president would later arouse a ripple of laughter from the audience when he referred to them as "workaholic staff members" in his inaugural speech.

The college's international emphasis was expressed in the Spanish used to offer greetings from Saint Michael's Latin American sister school representative. This speaker exemplified the community connections of Saint Michael's beyond the college's walls—to other higher education institutions, the state, the United States, and a global citizenry.

The faithful alumni were heralded as thirteen thousand strong and growing. Though infrequent campus visitors and only tangentially involved in the community, alumni represent the past, present, and future of the college. Alumni presence assures all that the college made it through past difficulties, including the founding and small student populations of the early days, and will surely continue to thrive.

The alumni who preceded the current undergraduates forged a path and, as such, hold an honored place within the community. As former students, alumni understand the institution from the inside out. This perspective affords a unique point of view of the college that faculty and staff can never completely understand. The alumni representative's voice shook ever so slightly as he welcomed the new president "into this special community."

Most notable among the greetings on this day was the testimony concerning the character of the man being inaugurated. Marc vanderHeyden was praised for being a "teacher with vision," a leader who could usher the college into a new century while remaining rooted in its past traditions. The informality of the college was mirrored in the use of his first name. His passion and enthusiasm for students, his accessible administrative style, and his sense of humor were widely acclaimed. In keeping with the spirit of hope and anticipation, speakers expressed their approval of this president who apparently understood the importance of student contact in this close-knit college community. Speaker after speaker introduced his or her remarks with comments about the president's understanding of student life. Since college presidents rarely have time for close contact with students, his tendency to converse and linger with students informally was considered worthy of comment. This was a community where students were central to the decisions and actions taken on behalf of the institution. The inauguration ceremony would not have been complete without students' presence as a constant reminder that the college exists in their name.

The board of trustees, the group that legally hires and fires the president, was conspicuously present at the inauguration. They, through different means from those of the institutional delegates, linked the college to the outside world of business, finance, and corporations. In addition to assuring the financial stability of the college, the board was responsible for stewarding the mission of the college and appointing its president. Similar to alumni, they straddled the domain between inside and outside with unique responsibilities concerning the institution. The board was represented by a 1974 alumnus and board member who reflected on the daunting task of filling the departing president's shoes. While the future of Saint Michael's College and higher education in general was uncertain and full of tumult, this alumnus board member was confident that the new president could rely on this "community of caring and faith."

The Musical Interlude

A musical interlude, following the last of the greetings and creating a pause or break in the ceremonial action, marked the end of one segment and the beginning of the next. The student wind ensemble reinforced the fact that during this ceremony the presence of student musicians was important. The dais party instinctively acknowledged the intention to honor members of the community by dutifully watching and listening to the wind ensemble for the duration of the interlude.

SYMBOLS

College rituals brim with symbols and meaning which are metaphors to represent something other than their literal meaning or appearance. The symbols used during the inauguration included the mace (symbolizing the president's role in protecting the institution), the college seal (reflecting the mission and founding), the presidential insignia or medallion (embodying the presidents who preceded the inaugural candidate), and the president himself (representing the institution).

Mace

The mace, a symbol of the office of the president is kept in the president's office, when it is not being used in a ceremony. During the inauguration ceremony at Saint Michael's College the mace was carried by the faculty marshal, a professor of English. The program explained: "The College mace is carried by the Grand Marshall in each academic procession . . . The head of the mace is crowned by a figure of Saint Michael the Archangel seated on the Earth, and the base of the staff features the cross of the Society of St. Edmund" (p. 23). A medieval symbol similar to regalia, the mace imparts on its presidential owner the responsibility of defending the institution.

Presidential Insignia or Medallion

During the investiture portion of the inauguration ceremony, the presidential medallion is placed around the president's neck. According to the inaugural program, this necklace is "worn by the President at formal academic events. It is a necklace bearing a large medallion depicting the official seal of the College. Along the chain upon which the medallion is suspended are smaller discs bearing the names and terms of office of all of the college presidents" (p. 23). The necklace was a gift of a former president of the institution.

College Seal

Latin phrases, original college names, depictions of the earliest campus buildings, references to institutional mottos, and founding dates are often contained on seals. The seal of Saint Michael's, depicted on the Inauguration program was the original seal of the college, purposely reintroduced for the ceremony. The round seal is bordered with Latin stating "Collegii S. Michaelis in Viridi Monte" or College of Saint Michael in the Green Mountains. Saint Michael the Archangel, his shield adorned with the fleurs de lis and scallop shells representing the college's founding order of French priests, adorns the seal's center. The saint holds a sword with which he had slain the dragon at his feet. The seal, similar to other such symbols, is stylized; the figure is not a literal representation but a figurative one.

President As Symbol

Presidents of colleges and universities are "institutional logos," stated one of the delegates. The presidential symbols, acclamations, and achievements cited marked the new president as distinctive. As the "institutional logo," the president is to be larger than life. His achievements must be more grand than the normal college professor. His leadership must confirm his competence, skill, and, in many cases, courage. But these symbolic representations of a larger-than-life figure must be accompanied actions that convey that he is also accessible to the community. The greeters in this inaugural ceremony straddled these two perspectives as if to say, "We want you to be extraordinary but we want you to be one of us."

THE INVESTITURE AND ROBING OF THE PRESIDENT

The climax of an inaugural ceremony is the investiture and robing of the incoming president. Shrouded with symbolic meaning and ritualistic actions, this point in the ceremony contains a tangible pivot. The president walks into the ceremony as an outsider, an incoming, but not quite a full-fledged member of the community. With the ceremonial robing and words spoken, Marc vanderHeyden actually *became* Saint Michael's president. The transformation did not occur with the search committee procedures, the salary negotiation, or the move to Vermont. The person *became* the president of the institution during the inauguration ceremony.

The investiture portion of an inaugural ceremony is executed differently across institutions. At large, public universities, the president is often invested by a chancellor or state system executive. At others, the chair of the board of trustees performs the ceremony. During the Saint Michael's College inauguration, three people were honored with the task of robing the president: the chairman of the board of trustees, the fourteenth and outgoing college president, and the president of the student association. The importance of community at this small New England college was illustrated in the choice of these three participants. The past president created a direct link between old and new leadership. The presence of the student association president communicated the central role students played in the college community. The board of trustees chair represented the group legally responsible for overseeing the president's hiring, firing, and actions. Together these three people and their roles linked the obligations and responsibilities present in the community with the president whose leadership expressed and represented that community.

For the robing, Dr. vanderHeyden removed his black academic robe and degree-coordinated hood to exchange it for a purple robe and a white hood. The use of a presidential, school color-coordinated robe was a twist on standard inaugural program proceedings. Initiated recently, "the use of the purple Presidential Robe began during the term of Dr. Paul J. Reiss, fourteenth president of Saint Michael's," according to the inaugural program. While the significance of this gesture can be easily exaggerated, it is consequential for an academic to exchange his robe, signifying his academic achievement and disciplinary expertise, and don non-discipline-associated regalia. In this case, the presidential robe was designed by the outgoing president and symbolized the institution, as indicated by the school colors, rather than any academic discipline.

Removing his personal regalia and adopting the purple robe of the president could be viewed as crossing a threshold from being an "ordinary" academic to becoming the president of the institution. Through this action, he became the ultimate symbol of the college. The symbols of the college presidency were bestowed on Marc vanderHeyden during the investiture portion of the ceremony: the presidential robe, presidential insignia or medallion, and charter of the institution. The insignia was placed around his neck, and he was handed the charter of Saint Michael's College. This individual wears the presidential robe, maintains the charter in safekeeping, and dons the necklace of the presidents. He is a symbol of all that occupying the office of the president entails.

The pivot point of academic becoming president was sealed with the following statement spoken by the chair of the board of trustees: "By the power vested in me by the Board of Trustees, I confer upon you the title of president of Saint Michael's College with all the rights and duties attended with that position." This phrase, familiar to all who have attended college graduations, supports the idea that the ceremony is not official—not complete—until these ritualistic words are uttered.

The Inaugural Speech

Inaugurations present an opportunity to promote a new mission, share knowledge about the history of the institution, and reinforce enduring truths about higher education. These messages, while expressed through the words of the greeters and the music of the student choir and ensemble, were most appropriately communicated in the inaugural speech delivered by Marc vanderHeyden.

Wearing the purple presidential robe and the presidential medallion, Marc vanderHeyden delivered his inaugural address. Speaking in a somewhat ponderous way that was neither boring nor tedious, his words indicated that he was a man who knew the importance of the task he had been hired to undertake. During his speech, he took his time in a deliberate, unhurried manner. The theatrical nature of the ceremony was not lost on this newly inaugurated president. The "thank you's" to the greeters and acknowledgments to the array of representatives were carefully delivered. He knew that this inaugural speech would set the tone for his college presidency. With four hundred students, alumni, faculty, staff, and local community members present, his words and intentions for this small liberal arts college would be carefully weighed. His deliberate, formal manner indicated someone who was savoring the moment—for himself and the community.

Saint Michael's link to a liberal arts tradition was illustrated through vanderHeyden's quotes from John Henry Cardinal Newman's, *The Idea of a University*. He vowed to an inventory of promises linked to the history, goals, and vision of his presidency. The Edmundite, liberal arts, and cultural traditions served as a framework for his thinking and practice. Nature, a crucial connection in this environmentally conscious state, served as inspiration. And, lastly, he promised "to be faithful to myself and the gifts given to me." He intended "to give back much of what has been given to me." Through these promises of faithfulness, he created a bridge to the college's past, linked that past to the issues of the current world, and situated his presidency in the Catholic tradition of the institution.

The new president knew that the college community was "confronted with the incredible task of making our type of education accessible to all." In uttering these words, he was not simply talking about money and tuition, although these concerns must have been on his mind. There was a sense that he was talking about how to make a high quality Christian-based education accessible to people who are not Christian or aligned with that tradition. How were people different from the predominantly Catholic, middle-class, traditional-aged college student to feel safe and supported within this closely knit community? How were they to arrive at Saint Michael's College in the first place? How do colleges in the "Catholic tradition" meet the challenges of providing a high quality education in a secular world? "Our type of education" may not be welcomed by all. "Our type" of institution does not always succeed with providing access. The challenge issued in the inaugural speech was to maintain tradition and the essential roots of the institution while opening that education to all in a just and fair manner.

Journeying through his speech back to the saint for whom the college was named, Dr. vanderHeyden concluded: "To build meaning into relationships is building meaning into life—including a genuine spiritual life. If we do it right, we will be like the archangels. That's where Saint Michael's is," he said while standing under the banner of the infamous archangel. New presidencies are a time for promises to be made to the community. Inaugural speeches must embody aspirations larger than any one individual. While college presidents can speak inspirational words on any occasion, an inauguration presents a more pronounced opportunity to express a new direction, forge a renewed vision, or update a sagging mission. Listening to the concluding words of this inaugural speech, one could imagine being pulled, through human efforts, into heaven to perform courageous acts in the name of God.

MESSAGES WITHIN THE INAUGURATION

Several themes concerning institutional history came into play during Saint Michael's Inauguration: institutional history and founding beliefs, the presence of many voices, the links to the community, differences, and stewardship.

Institutional History and Founding Beliefs

Community-wide ceremonies such as inaugurations, commencements, and founder's days retell institutional history and beliefs. This declaration of history, not hollow words spoken in a pro forma manner, injects value in the listeners and meaning into the words. The act is mutually shaping. Listeners come to believe and live the history; the history remains alive in the lives of the listeners. As such, individual histories become communal history; communal history becomes individual history.

Presence of Many Voices

This inaugural ceremony was characterized by many voices: Canadian accented French greetings, a Belgian-accented inaugural speech, Spanish from the Latin American sister school representative, and Latin from the Bishop of Vermont. The message conveyed was that languages other than English were to be spoken. The fact that not everyone understood the language was not a reason for the words to go unspoken because during ceremony, meaning can be conveyed beyond words. And in a true community, many voices are to be spoken—and heard. The man being inaugurated acknowledged this community need and desire through a reference during his inaugural speech to "the fine art of listening." This statement reinforced the previous speaker's comments about his openness and ability to listen to various campus constituencies, an essential skill in this close community.

The message of community emanating from all these voices was the desire for a leader who would listen. Given the complexity of the voices—the religiously oriented past, the tuition-concerned parents, the fun-loving students, the business-oriented board of trustees—this task of listening was a difficult one. Inherent in the listening—and the speaking—was the danger of miscommunication.

Link to Community

Over and over again in word and action, speakers and participants communicated their connection or "solidarity" to the institution and their commitment to its purposes. An aspect of living virtuously in community is the obligation members have toward each other. Specifically, educated people have an obligation to share their talent and gifts with others. This sharing is not an empty exercise but a way of living virtuously. Knowledge and skills can be used to create a better world than the one in which they currently live. "Men are not just social animals but spiritual beings," said Dr. vanderHeyden.

Difference

Reflecting the president's words about wanting "our students to break out of the insularity that is not moral," there was an effort to honor differences through the presence of a range and diversity of ceremony participants. Decades earlier, the leadership of the college recognized that the community would have to become more inclusive in an ecumenical sense in order to fulfill its mission as a higher education institution. The inaugural speech reflected these intentions as Dr. vanderHeyden drew upon traditional references to the Catholic Church while creating a bridge between those traditional ideas and the needs of the community to be more inclusive. He acknowledged the difficulty though necessity of fulfilling this purpose.

One of the means to achieve this goal was through the international programs and the students who participated in them. They created a global presence that stood in stark contrast to the homogeneity of the student body and the state of Vermont. The new president was offering a challenge to this insular community to become something more than what they already were.

Stewardship

Stewardship of the community in the form of leadership was a significant theme within the inauguration. The president, in particular, discussed stewardship as related to his gifts. Through his inaugural speech the new president discussed his desire to bestow his talents upon the college. This conspicuous acknowledgment of his abilities was not effected in a self-centered or self-involved manner. Instead, the president discussed the need to recognize one's individual gifts in order to give those gifts back to the community. Gifts are the link between service and community.

Mentors, family, and friends are responsible for helping us recognize, foster, and express our gifts in the most ethical means possible as these gifts are realized through our actions with others. Because gifts emerge in community, we are obligated to return those gifts to the communities in which they were nurtured.

METAPHORS WITHIN THE CEREMONY

Metaphors and analogies are often used extensively during rituals and ceremonies to convey content not easily expressed through more direct means. During the inauguration, the metaphors of bridge, light, and journey were used prominently to express the vision and mission of the institution.

Bridge

The bridge metaphor was used to discuss time and history. This metaphor was particularly useful as the ceremony participants paid homage to past college leadership. The metaphor of the bridge, a symbol of continuity from old to new, was a fitting way to honor the founders and past leadership. Stories were told about the founding Edmundite priests, the founding document was read in its original language, and past and present leaders were acknowledged with a place of honor on the dais. In fact, any shortcomings possessed by past leaders were ignored, overlooked, or just not mentioned as this was an occasion to celebrate achievement—past and anticipated.

The use of the word bridge, and the expression of continuity that this metaphor symbolizes, communicated the community's hope for the next steps to be taken under new presidential leadership. Each new college leader would use his or her gifts to assist the institution in progressing to the next step of its development. Standing on the shoulders of giants, each new leader would guide the institution in concert with the needs of the community.

The hope, symbolized in the bridge metaphor, built anticipation. At its very core, the inauguration expressed pride about where the community had been, honored the founders who had the vision to forge that path, reinforced beliefs guiding the institution, and engendered hope that they would rise to even greater accomplishments in the future.

Light

Light as a symbol communicated how this modern college linked itself to its ancient Catholic tradition. This link was particularly established through the presence of Edmundite community members. They were a living symbol of the institution's legacy still present within the community. The founding proclamation was read by the local superior of the Edmundite priests in its original handwritten French. A significant document for this community, the proclamation was written in 1904, on the anniversary of St. Michael the Archangel and the founding date of the college.

While the college had evolved from its religious founding to a more nonsectarian existence, the presence of the Catholic tradition was undeniable. But one did not hear the words "Catholic college" being spoken from the inaugural podium. Instead, "in the Catholic tradition" or "in light of the Catholic faith" (literally lifted from the college's mission statement) were substituted as a more subdued, inclusive version of its roots as a Catholic institution.

Journey

The religious affiliation of the institution offered another powerful metaphor for use throughout the inauguration: journey. This metaphor was a familiar one in this Catholic community accustomed to parables, gospels, and accounts of Christ's travels. The arrival of a new president became an opportunity to link the journey from the past, through the present, and into the future. "I chose a rather convoluted path to come to Saint Michael's but one I do not regret and one for which I will be forever grateful. I believe my habit of being a perennial student has been a good preparation for becoming president of this prestigious institution."

The new president's personal journey to this unforeseen leadership position began, unknowingly, as a monk. The presidential search committee had found a college president of two worlds: the traditional monastic world of the college's past and the newer secular world of the future. His success as a leader of this religiously affiliated community would depend on his talent for straddling both worlds. The former was characterized by spirituality and the life of the mind; the latter by balanced budgets, curriculum relevant to the world's demands, and student recruitment and retention. He reflected upon the similarities of the two: the interior solitude necessary for a monk and college president, the integrity needed in both roles. According to this college leader, one needs solitude and reflection to accept a leadership role.

Though obviously a person with years of professional work ahead of him, Marc vanderHeyden spoke about his term as the president of Saint Michael's College as the end of his career journey. By linking his destiny with that of the college, he communicated his commitment and attachment to the institution. This was the place he had chosen to fulfill his career goals. This institution was an intimate part of his life, not a stepping-stone to another presidency at a larger institution. He started his journey as a monk and ended it as a college president.

BENEDICTION

The ceremony was brought to an end with a benediction performed by a priest and a rabbi. The rabbi was local and well known for his community activism and commitment to social justice causes. The Edmundite priest, an African American man, was a bishop and 1954 alumnus of Saint Michael's.

In keeping with the diversity theme and to acknowledge the rabbi's determination to attend the ceremony, the master of ceremonies introduced him by noting that because it was the Sabbath and the Orthodox Jew was forbidden by religious law from driving. The rabbi had walked miles to attend the inauguration. To participate in community, sacrifices would have to be made. The rabbi praised Saint Michael's College as a "remarkable community of faith."

RECEPTION FOLLOWING THE CEREMONY

A reception was held after the ceremony on the college green. Participants in the inauguration could greet the new president, his wife, and other members of the platform party via a receiving line assembled on the library steps. Students, faculty, administrators, and community members milled around the lawn, ate cookies, and drank punch. Well-wishers snaked across the steps and down the sidewalk.

Marc vanderHeyden, standing at the end of the line, appeared overwhelmed by the events in which he had just participated. So many people to meet, so many hands to shake, so many faces to remember.

The weather had turned cold and a rainstorm had blown in. Living in Vermont was for the hardy. But the warmth of this college community would counter any adverse weather for the new president and his administration.

Chapter 3

Rites of Passage: Structuralism

> Upon entering ritual space they [participants] enter a domain distinct from the quotidian and do so in order to reenact an ancient story or pattern. Ritual entertains complex relations with what is outside it. But this bracketing, this *existence within quotation marks* is clearly a serious categorical bracketing that cannot be tinkered with (Morgan, 1984, p. 82).

Structuralism, until the rise of postmodernism, was a dominant theoretical perspective in anthropological thought. Articulated by Claude Levi-Strauss (1955), structuralism was originally proposed as a methodology but steadily became an anthropological ideology. The basic tenet of structuralism is that "operations [are] performed by the human mind in general, not just . . . particular minds at particular times" (Sturrock, 1979, p. 4). In structuralism, priority is given to universal ideals and principles rather than individual needs and ideas (Orphanides, 1992). Through the use of structuralist theory, cultural phenomena can be understood as resting on a few abstract universal principles and cognitive structures (DeFlem, 1991; Ortner, 1984) that hold constant across cultures, contexts, time, and history. Some of these universals include hierarchy, transformation, regeneration, and development.

Structuralists assume that there is an inherent, natural order to culture. This order is uncovered through the anthropological study of social lives, organizations, myths, and rituals. Ritual theory, for example, highlights the relationship between universal human needs (community, love, family). Ritual calls attention to these needs, assist us to see the relationships between and among them, and remind us of their importance.

STRUCTURALISM AND HIGHER EDUCATION RITUALS

This chapter, therefore, briefly summarizes rites of passage structure, functions of rites of passage, and universal beliefs embodied within them. The chapter concludes with observations concerning structuralism's strengths and weaknesses as regards rituals.

An explanation of the structuralist theory of ritual is important in the context of this book for three reasons: (1) Rites of passage and the transformation they evoke, remain a common term between ritual participants and planners. (2)

Structuralist theory, particularly as outlined by Arnold van Gennep (1960), can lead to a better understanding of the organization, process, and logistics of rituals. (3) The structuralist ritual theory concept of liminality, particularly as expanded by post-structuralist Victor Turner (see chapter 7), accommodates a powerful symbolic and functional explanation concerning ritual action.

RITES OF PASSAGE

Ritual emerged in the nineteenth century as a term to identify what was theorized as a "universal category of human experience" (Bell, 1992, p. 14). Van Gennep (1960) established ritual as a topic of study with his classic, *The Rites of Passage*. Rites of passage are defined as "ceremonies whose essential purpose is to enable the individual to pass from one defined position to another which is equally well-defined" (p. 3). The use of the word "pass" in this definition alludes to the processual nature of van Gennep's rites of passage (DeFlem, 1991). According to van Gennep, rites of passage can occur with any change of physiology, place, or social status. Because these changes create disturbances in the cultural group, rites of passages reestablish the equilibrium and reduce the harm.

While van Gennep defined rites of passage within non-Western cultures, "there is no evidence that a secularized urban world has lessened the need for ritualized expression of an individual's transition from one status to another" (1960, p. xxii). People in postmodern, postindustrial communities such as colleges and universities, educated in the scientific tradition, may claim that rituals are no longer needed. Ritual from this cynical perspective is an "empty gesture" (McLaren, 1986, p. 17) lacking "efficacy—or even . . . existence . . . in modern, mainstream life" (p. 19).

Prior to my observations and research on rituals in higher education, I, too, believed that rituals were an anachronistic part of college life. I postulated that college students treated rituals as a necessary evil—a part of campus life that was, at best, tolerated and, at worst, boring. To my surprise I found that while students often called the rituals "stupid" or "corny," they also felt they were an integral part of college life.

Therefore, higher education institutions, the context for this book, have rituals such as inaugurations, graduations, and convocations that meet van Gennep's definition of rites of passage. During these activities, a person passes from one stage or status to another (nonpresident to president; student to graduate; newcomer to community member) because of the ritual action. The ritual subjects (also called initiates, neophytes, or liminars), performers, and spectators (Daly, 1990; Kapferer, 1984; Turner, V., 1967) attend rituals endowed with meaning and steeped in tradition.

Rite of passage theory maintains that these events are not simply reenactments or symbolic representations of the change in status. Rites of passage *are* the place where the change actually occurs. For example, as illustrated in the inauguration case study contained in this book, the incoming president did not become the president as a result of screening committee action, salary negotiation, or arrival on campus. He *became* the president of St. Michael's College *during* the inauguration rite, specifically during the investiture within the ceremony.

Rites of Passage Structure

Van Gennep (1960) theorized that rituals have a consistent structure regardless of the culture or function (Turner, T., 1977). "Only in form do the rites vary according to peoples and kinds of restricted groups" (van Gennep, p. 302). Rites of passage, by definition, are composed of an inherent three-part structure: separation (preliminal), transition (liminal), and incorporation (postliminal).

Separation Stage. During this first stage, the ritual participant is disconnected, metaphorically or physically, from his or her present social state. This separation signals the start of the rite of passage, indicates the distinctiveness of the participants, and positions them for the impending change. "Separation comprises symbolic behavior signifying the detachment of the individual or group either from an earlier fixed point in the social structure or a set of cultural conditions" (Turner, V., 1967, p. 94). Time and place are specially set aside and accentuated to temporarily disconnect the ritual participants from their community. This separation marks them as special: they are the people for whom the ceremony was organized. Prior to the commencement processional, college graduates-to-be are separated from family, faculty, and other members of the college community. They line up together, struggle with the unfamiliar regalia, and walk as one into the ceremony.

Transition or Liminal Stage. The second stage, transition or liminal, is ambiguous, paradoxical, and dangerous. The liminal stage is the most enigmatic of rites of passage stages. During this stage, the participant has "few or none of the attributes of the past or coming state" (Turner, V., 1967, p. 94). This transition state endows these rites of passage with the "ability to *transform* participants into different social statuses as well as different states of consciousness" (McLaren, 1986, p. 46). This is the time and place where change occurs.

The transition or liminal stage is mysterious and dangerous because the ritual participant lies suspended between old and new states. During this liminal stage, there occurs the "emergence of society's deepest values in the form of sacred dramas and objects—sometimes the reenactment periodically of cosmogonic narratives or deeds of saintly, godly, or heroic establishers of morality, basic intuitions, or ways of approaching transcendent beings or powers" (Turner, V., 1984, p. 22). Victor Turner (1967) described this stage as "betwixt and between"; you are neither here nor there; it is "in and out of time" (1974, p. 197). The ambiguity of being between cultural states (e.g., no longer a senior but not quite a graduate) is confusing and unsafe. As human beings, we want such ambiguity resolved. "Because the liminal stage contains such dramatic movement, it is wide open to endless possibilities. It discloses "a 'realm of possibility' where new combinations of cultural givens could be playfully tested. Liminal situations . . . were, thus, 'seedbeds of cultural creativity,' giving rise to new ideas and new paradigms" (Ashley, 1990, p. xviii).

During the liminal stage (from *limen* which is Latin for threshold) (Turner, V., 1974), there is a portal or space through which the ritual participant passes. Standing on the edge of the portal, the participant glimpses the world into which he or she is to be admitted. At a certain point in the ceremony, complete with ritualistic language, symbolism, and action, the portal opens and the participant must choose whether or not to pass. This transition may be symbolized by the act of changing the initiate's name (Turner, V., 1967), through a change of clothing, or a special incantation. Senior students become graduates when the president of the college intones, "By the power vested in me . . . ." With a switch of the tassels from left to right, they have changed from one state to another.

By techniques van Gennep called magic, the person involved adopts a sacred role. For example, during inaugurations, a ceremony originally for kings and queens, exalted status is conferred on the president. He or she is granted special rights within the community. Even as the first among equals in the collegial setting of higher education, the presidential role carries significant weight. There are very few, if any, activities similar to rites of passage that can confer such significance to an individual or group.

Incorporation Stage. The third stage, incorporation, welcomes the rite of passage participants back into the community. The danger has passed and the person is merged back into the culture with the rights and privileges of his or her new role. In this final stage of rites of passage, "the passage is consummated. The ritual subject, individual or corporate, is in a stable state once more and, by virtue of this, has rights and obligations of a clearly defined and 'structural' type, and is expected to behave in accordance with certain customary norms and ethical standards" (Turner, V., 1967, p. 94).

Participants of rites of passage are so adapted to their well-established structure that the form is taken for granted. The structure is virtually invisible within the pacing of the ceremony; one expects the separation, anticipates the climax, and knows that the action will ebb to a conclusion.

Without rituals, there would be nothing to mark this cultural change in status as extraordinary. There would be less meaning created for individuals and within communities because these inexplicable changes would be treated as commonplace.

Higher education is particularly replete with rituals and rites of passage that mark changes in status. One can speculate that these rituals are so abundant in colleges and universities because the work performed is not visible. The acquisition of an education, the conferral of a degree, and the achievement of a goal would remain less real without rituals to endow them with meaning.

Functions of Rites of Passage

Similar to the predictable, familiar structure, rites of passage fulfill purposes which only they are uniquely meant to achieve. These functions are as familiar and predictable as the well-known structure. Among others, they (a) express primordial needs, (b) mark cyclical milestones, (c) allow us to negotiate paradox and confusion, (d) express magic, and (e) allot time and opportunity for reflection. We expect these purposes so automatically that empty feelings result if the ritual is missed, fails to occur, or, even worse, misfires (Moore & Myerhoff, 1977). Missed graduations, sparsely attended convocations, and poorly run inaugurations are foregone opportunities to create new possibilities, reflect on and reformulate roles, and celebrate achievements.

Express Primordial Needs. Whether based on the longevity within human communities or the feelings evoked through their action, rituals occupy a central place in culture building. Rituals possess a primordial and vital character by appealing to the place within human beings where culture is created, stored, and reenacted. This character is especially true when rituals are used, and they nearly always are, to convey messages not easily communicated in everyday language. When one is talking about the highest possible academic achievement, necessity of women's and people of color's success, power of leadership, and profound gift of self to a community, rituals are an extremely powerful mode of communication. There is, as McLaren pointed out, an "epistemological nobility" (1986, p. 20) about rituals. We come to know the meaning they embody by taking part and/or talking about their action. The knowledge communicated in rituals is unique to this cultural form.

Mark Cyclical Milestones. Their primordial character enables rites of passage to convincingly mark natural and periodic cycles, the milestones of one's life. Seasonal rites such as founder's days in the fall and community picnics in the spring are performed at well-defined points in the annual cycle. While van Gennep theorized about the cyclically occurring puberty, purification, and healing rites to ensure fertility, protection, and reincarnation, cyclical campus rites of passage take a different form. A tree planting can attest to the longevity and endurance of higher education. Mountain Day at Mount Holyoke College celebrates the beauty of New England autumns (Manning, 1989a). Winter Carnival at Dartmouth College celebrates rather than laments the long, cold winters. Fountain Day at the University at Albany announces that spring, at long last, has arrived.

At Mount Holyoke College, seasonal changes, clearly marked through changes in the grounds and buildings, could be noted, regardless of the weather, by traditions that occurred like clockwork. Students understood the sense of purpose and faith created by the fact that, regardless of what happened within the college and in higher education, those traditions, as they called them, would surely prevail (Manning, 1989a).

Negotiate Paradox and Confusion. Rites of passage, as briefly discussed above, stimulate ambiguity, uncertainty, and paradox. Unfettered by the everyday structures of daily living, the participant is free to ponder "alternative social possibilities" (Ashley, 1990, p. xx). The disconnection from the past life creates an ambiguity during which anything is possible. Faced with a series of diametrically opposed concepts (self and other, community and individual, past and present, in and out, night and day), myriads of choices are possible between the continua ends (Babcock, 1990; Daly, 1990). "The liminal adolescent—no longer a child, not yet an adult—is free to contemplate a multiplicity of possible adulthoods. Indeed, the anxiety attendant upon this condition is often balanced by an exhilaration in the freedom it affords" (Daly, p. 71).

With freedom comes danger as these participants threaten themselves and the group order. With the social roles and conventions removed, they could concoct an unacceptable role. Ritual, in its remarkably ambiguous way, creates danger while simultaneously controlling it. The fact that ritual occurs in the first place means that certain behaviors, based on past history and cultural practice, are encouraged. The prescribed behaviors and expected action can promote social control by presenting the participant with a limited number of possible models. In other words, while everything from black to white on the continuum is theoretically possible, only certain roles are culturally sanctioned. Ritual opens and closes possibilities simultaneously.

Marching into a college's commencement ceremony, the senior glimpses the person he or she might become. Models of this transformation abound: the faculty in regalia, family members with college degrees, administrators with careers entrenched in higher education. During the ceremony, if they choose, they could become the person sighted. But danger exists in the time and place of this choice. During graduations, students adorn their mortar boards with political messages, dress in shorts and sneakers unbefitting the formal occasion, and drink champagne to excess. Poised at the cusp between student and adulthood, these activities are dangerous to the community. Will the graduates accept their adult roles or continue to play adolescent games? The transformation is complete when the danger created during the rite of passage is skirted and the culturally sanctioned choice of roles is made. But a complete understanding of ritual compels one to believe that the safe choices made can be as dangerous to the long-term health of the culture as the hazardous ones.

Perhaps a major difference between non-Western, traditional rites of passage such as the ones van Gennep (1960) studied and those common on college campuses is the choice available to participants. In traditional cultures, the transformation to be achieved during the ceremony is largely predetermined. In democratic, Western cultures such as the United States, the participant has more choice about the role into which he or she will transform (Turner, V., 1972). Rather than one or two choices, the participant, during the ritual, can reflect upon an array of choices open to him or her at that moment. The importance of this decision clearly weighs heavy on students' minds as they experience anxiety, push to make career decisions, and hurry to find the consummate postcollege job.

Express Magic. Through their out-of-the-ordinary action, their call to uncommon themes, and their capacity to link participants to the lofty aspects of human existence, rituals are magical. Ritual, link people to events, history, and a world larger than the confines of their existence. Because they "unfold in 'spaces' clearly differentiated from those of everyday discourse or action; they are . . . inscribed within the realm of possibility and make-believe" (Morgan, 1984, p. 79). Ritual's surreal, magical quality can be used, scrupulously and unscrupulously, to convince people of realities that may or may not be true. Through magic, a community can achieve purposes beyond the realities that it must, at some point, face.

Allow Reflection. During rites of passage, with an opening of possibilities and bracketing of time and space, people are free to contemplate, not only their lives up until that moment, but their existence from then on. In

the liminal periods of major *rites of passage* the . . . [participants] are free . . . to contemplate for a while the mysteries that confront all men [*sic*], the

> difficulties that peculiarly beset their own society, their personal problems, and the ways in which their own wisest predecessors have sought to order, explain, explain away, cloak, or mask . . . mysteries and difficulties (Turner, V., 1974, pp. 241-242).

During rites of passage, participants can reflect upon their community, world, and the powers that sustain their existence (Turner, V., 1967, p. 105).

Perhaps on college campuses the faculty and administrators have underestimated the weightiness of the decisions faced by students during rites of passage. The student, new to the challenge of defining his or her adult role, benefits from both earnest reflection and the practice of weighty decision making. The ancient form of rituals informs college participants that these events create space for and present a form that mediates this decision making. Ritual marks the students' reflection and late adolescent distress as an aspect of life to be taken seriously. The grander the ritual, the more participants communicate that these decisions have consequences on culture and community. Their individual actions are nothing less than a continual and regenerative shaping of the beliefs and tenets of culture.

SACRED AND UNIVERSAL BELIEFS

Emile Durkheim, an early structuralist, linked religion and other universal belief systems to ritual (1915). Religion, composed of beliefs and doctrine, employed ritual as a "means by which collective beliefs and ideals are simultaneously generated, experienced, and affirmed as real by the community. Hence, ritual is the means by which individual perception and behavior are socially appropriated or conditioned" (Ashley, 1990, p. 20). Ritual forms a dialectic between the communal and individual and the universal and particular. Several universal beliefs, as defined by the structuralists, explored through ritual include (a) transcendence, (b) regeneration, and (c) death and rebirth.

Transcendence

Rites of passage as described by van Gennep were based on religious and universal beliefs. Religion was the underlying theory, and magic defined the practice. Universal beliefs such as deity worship, human bonding, and ancestor relevance were some of the bases of rituals to bless a new home, initiate new members, and reenact ancient journeys. Rites of passage mark occasions of naming, initiation, and other first-time events (Turner, V., 1969, 1977b; van Gennep, 1960).

Although most colleges in the United States are secular, the religious nature of institutional life remains firmly embedded in higher education rituals. The most significant vestige of the sacred nature of campus ritual life is academic regalia. Originating in medieval times, regalia harkens back to the monastic tradition. During graduate student hooding ceremonies, regalia is bestowed by an academic on graduating masters and doctoral students. This action symbolizes the handing over and acceptance of the "sacra" (van Gennep, 1960). The already established academic bestows the honor and obligations of status as an educated person upon the graduating student. The solemnness of the ceremony as well as the use of these almost holy vestments engenders meaning and significance upon the ritual action. Rituals call upon participants' spiritual selves, creating a commonality of purpose, understanding, and sacredness. "Rituals are imperishably rooted in man's [sic] search for transcendence. They provide for contemporary man dimensions to his existence which have been termed symbolic, holy, mythic or poetic" (McLaren, 1986, p. 38). Rituals draw upon humans' spiritual quest. For college students this quest may be represented by a yearning to link their individual lives to larger purposes. Community values, enacted during rituals, inspiring this quest may include volunteerism, leadership, and the obligations of educated people to improve the human condition. Spiritual unity is created through ritual action by opening a space where community members come together, not only in physical proximity, but in an intersection of action, beliefs, and meaning.

Regeneration

Reflecting the weightiness of universal human values, van Gennep's conception of the importance of ritual is essentially boundless. Ritual, he believed, is intimately bound to regeneration, a universal law of life. Like the natural world, the social world has to regenerate itself to survive. This process occurs through rites of passage that mimic the cyclical changes in nature. The idea that rites of passage are connected to social life regeneration places those events at the very heart of human action. The theory links rituals to magic, spiritualism, and nature.

Regeneration corresponds unerringly to the belief structures of college campuses. Particularly with the expanded numbers of non-traditionally aged students and varied approaches to receiving a higher education, colleges are communities that regenerate themselves through a constant infusion of newcomers. New students are incorporated into the community each semester. The community is renewed and re-created through an everchanging flow of new faces. Furthermore, as a community where intellectual exploration is standard practice, founding beliefs and fundamental values are questioned, examined, and, when necessary, discarded or re-created.

Death and Rebirth

Regeneration as a universal value is linked to death and rebirth. These latter concepts, adapted from nature, are an integral part of community life. Rites of passage symbolize these inevitable processes through the separation (death) and reincorporation (rebirth) stages. In the transition state, liminars are "betwixt and between" the structural roles prescribed by society. The neophytes are neither living nor dead from one aspect, and both living and dead from another. "Their condition is one of ambiguity and paradox, a confusion of all the customary categories" (Turner, V. 1967, p. 97).

In the inauguration at Saint Michael's College, the incoming president removed his academic regalia that represented his discipline and degree-granting institution. Upon removing the symbols of his former affiliation, he donned the purple robe of the president of Saint Michael's College. His former academic self, though not completely eradicated, was symbolically replaced, at least for the period of his term, with his new life as president. Such ceremonial donning of regalia symbolizes the death of an old role and adoption of a new. The de-robing symbolizes the fact that the new president has nothing—"no status, insignia, secular clothing, rank" (Turner, V., 1967, p. 98-99). Any previous status must be removed or die in order to make room for the new.

STRUCTURALISM, HIGHER EDUCATION, AND RITES OF PASSAGE

While structuralism has largely been discredited as a theoretical perspective and replaced by postmodernism, vestiges of structuralist ideas abound in higher education. The perspective adopted in this book and upon which this ritual research was based is that culture is socially constructed. Belief systems, even so-called universal ones, are socially constructed by humans. Universals are labeled as such as a result of human action. Even such universals as nature are viewed through the lens of human action and cultural beliefs. With this in mind, the following sections explore the strengths and weaknesses of structuralism and posit its usefulness and lack thereof as a theoretical structure to understand higher education rituals.

Using Structuralism to Understand Higher Education Rituals

Van Gennep's theory of rites of passage can assist observers of higher education rituals to understand that there *is* an order to social life that can be discerned. Human actors do not live in a vacuum but rather base their present behaviors on models from the past. These models are often presented in dramatic and highly stylized forms through rituals. Incoming students learn the expectations of academic life through the speeches, processions, and symbols of convocation. These students do not invent their academic behavior anew but rather base it on models—helpful and not so helpful—that already exist within the campus community.

Structuralism can also assist one to recognize the powerful structural forces underlying rituals and other social experiences. The difference between structure as defined by the structuralists and the approach employed in this book is a belief that structure is neither an inherent nor natural force completely independent of human behavior. Rather, structure, socially constructed, is created through the action of human beings.

Van Gennep's theories can assist one to consider how rites of passage focus human action as people pass from late adolescence to adulthood, students to graduates, and college world to outside world participants. Homecomings can be understood as rites of reincarnation, convocations as rites of initiation, student performances as rites of inversion, Greek rituals as rites of resistance, and founder's days as rites of founding (McLaren, 1986). Gatherings of the college community become rites of solidarity. Community-wide meetings mark life crises. College couples return to university chapels to perform marriage rites. Memorial services as death rites are commonplace on college campuses. Religiously affiliated campuses are particularly apt to conduct curative rituals. (See table 1, chapter 1.)

The Ways Structuralism Is Unhelpful

Structuralism and van Gennep's rites of passage theory are unhelpful in understanding rituals for several reasons. The (a) underlying determinism of the theory, (b) non-Western perspective, (c) lack of contextual analysis and flexibility, and (d) inability to explain individual diversity, change, and complexity make the theory an incomplete explanation of the intricacies of today's college rituals. Van Gennep's belief in an inherent structure is limiting as one considers the context dependent, historically based community in which college rituals and ceremonies occur.

Determinism. The deterministic paradigm that underscores structuralism states that rituals, in part, reinforce social ties, express social conflicts, and delineate social roles. In short, there is a predetermined order served by rituals regardless of the participants involved. In contrast to van Gennep's deterministic functions for rituals, the theory advanced in this book contends that rituals fulfill undetermined, spontaneous, and unintended purposes as well as those imagined by the ritual planners or posited by deterministic structuralists. For some ritual participants, the rituals are just plain fun or, for other participants, have no purpose at all.

Non-Western Perspective. Structuralist theory, based on non-Western rituals, in general was insufficient for a focus on Western rituals. One cannot significantly change contexts without changing the nature of the phenomenon being discussed. In other words, non-Western (e.g., African tribal rituals) cannot be taken out of context and applied indiscriminately to a Western, postindustrial context (e.g., college campus) without distorting an understanding of the traditions and cultures of both settings.

Lack of Context and Inflexibility. Structuralist theory's underlying assumption of universal similarity of structures does not allow enough flexibility when one considers American higher education, which is characterized by diversity (public/private, mission, and quality) and lack of uniformity. The static, universal model of structuralism does not explain the diverse character of higher education institutions nor the diversity of the people who fill those institutions. The individuality and uniqueness of these people assure that the messages of ritual will be filtered through their perspectives and acquire very different meanings than those intended by the ritual planners.

Colleges and universities express their diversity through unique histories, ways of operating, and traditions. Given the diversity and individual history of colleges and universities, one cannot assume that even the most basic, fundamental structure is similar across institution-specific rituals. Rather than presuming that rituals adhere to a universal structure unrelated to the institution's history, I assume that a college's character significantly colors the structure and practice of the campus's rituals.

Assumption of Similarity. The underlying structuralist premise of similarity across cultures does not afford the flexibility needed to explain institutional change. Change occurs as a result of disparate interpretations of institutional ideologies and events. The structuralist model with its deterministic stance and unyielding structure cannot explain why, over time, structures, meanings, and perspectives evolve. Structuralism ignores faux pas, varied enactments, individual taste, current expediencies, and other factors that change the ritual over time.

Finally, structuralism does not help build a framework to understand the complex character of higher education institutions. Similarity of structure cannot explain the evolution and existence of institutions that serve a wide variety of internal and external constituencies, embody disparate—often paradoxical—purposes and attempt to serve ambiguous expectations from public and governmental sources.

Given the diversity of types of higher education, the idiosyncratic development of students, and the complexity of institutional functioning, one cannot assume that the circumstances operating in one institution coincide with the circumstances of another (Weick, 1979). Any similarity of functioning could be coincidence. Rather than similarity of structure and meaning, idiosyncratic interpretation and individualized action are, most likely, the norm.

SUMMARY

Rituals fulfill primordial, fundamental human needs. While a structuralist approach, as summarized in this chapter, offers some explanation for ritual practice, its shortcomings cannot conceal the fact that human beings need ritual in order to live in their communities. Rituals' ability to tap into our spiritual and transcendent side makes them an extremely important human activity. Their abundant presence on college campuses makes an argument for their importance even more convincing.

Chapter 4

Charter Day

The founder "would be proud."

—Secretary of the college

GRACIOUS DINING

Precisely at 6:15 p.m. on Charter Day, the women in the dormitory dining hall rose to their feet and sang Mount Holyoke's all-familiar alma mater. Most sang from memory, ignoring the lyrics printed and placed at their table setting. There was no need for assistance; the words and tune were well known. One hundred years ago to the day and minute, a charter, signed by the governor, arrived in South Hadley to proclaim the fifty-year-old seminary a college.

Charter Day is celebrated annually on March 8. Most years, the celebration is an inconsequential event but this year the Sesquicentennial Committee organized an event to commemorate the one hundred and fifty years of Mount Holyoke's existence as a college and the one hundredth anniversary of the charter's arrival.

Faculty members, responding to an appeal from the Sesquicentennial Committee, accepted the invitation to the "Gracious Dinners." College professors had been invited to these special monthly dinners since the 1920s when the faculty was predominantly single women. In those days, dinners were a time to don more formal clothes and engage in intellectual conversation. T-shirts, sweats, and jeans were currently the preferred attire among students. The dresses that traditionally marked Gracious Dining in the past were nowhere in sight.

Gracious Dining now meant that the regular dining hall food, minimally changed in quantity and variety, was served on tablecloths placed over the antique dining room tables. Polite after-dinner conversation over coffee was replaced by before-dinner wine and cheese served in the dormitory's elegant parlor. The change in practice complemented the intentions of Gracious Dining as each parlor was furnished with antique wing chairs, a fireplace, grandfather clock, and a grand piano.

THE SESQUICENTENNIAL

A sesquicentennial, one hundred and fifty years of women's higher education, and one hundred years as a chartered college were occasions worthy of celebration.

But the circumstances of the charter's arrival added to the lore of the college's auspicious founding. Historic accounts, often reaching mythical proportions, told of the founder's effort to establish the college: Mary Lyon's treks through the countryside to raise money for a female seminary, her remarkable effort to plan and open the college in an unprecedented three years, and her ability to take ideas from the best education available in her day and forge a prophetic vision of excellence. One hundred and fifty years of history were recited in speeches, passed down through storytelling, and reinforced in the very art and architecture of the college.

THE ILLUMINATION

According to letters and descriptions resurrected from the archives and exhibited in the library's glass display cases, a blizzard occurred in 1888 on the day the charter was to be delivered. The snow isolated the campus, delaying the charter's arrival. Upon its belated arrival, the charter was welcomed with an "Illumination." Candles, a valuable commodity for this frugal campus during the 1880s, adorned the seminary's windows to announce that a momentous circumstance had occurred.

For Charter Day's re-creation of the original Illumination, floodlights were trained on the administration building bearing the founder's name; electric candles lit every window. In advance of the events planned for Charter Day, students snickered about the Sesquicentennial Committee's plans for a popular history professor to re-create the charter's arrival on horseback. Regardless of the fun poked by the skeptics, the plans proceeded.

A Community's Strength

Students, administrators, and faculty stood in the alternating glare and shadow of the floodlights. The students greeted each other with their customary hugs and laughter. The strength of this college community did not emanate from any one group gathered that night on the muddy lawn of the administration building, the site of the original Illumination. No one group alone could perpetuate its traditions. Alumnae were external to the everyday business of the college; students lacked long-term, daily interaction with the college; and most administrators and faculty members had not experienced the college as students. Consistent and respectful interactions among faculty, students, alumnae, and administrators lent the college its unique and intense communal strength. All groups were needed to keep its spirit alive.

The Charter's Arrival

Excitement rippled through the crowd when the sound of galloping hooves was heard. Cries of "There he is" erupted as a rider in period dress carrying a rolled-up charter appeared. Bursting through the college's gates and riding toward the crowd, the horse, spooked by the cheers and applause, reared back. The professor, an accomplished rider, urged the horse back on course so that they could discharge their delivery. Despite his skill, horse and rider overshot the director of the Sesquicentennial poised to receive the charter. The founder "would be proud," this nonalumna administrator said, as she retrieved the runaway charter and led a second rendition of the alma mater. The dark was pierced with camera flashes as students documented yet another tradition in their college experience.

PRESENTATIONS AND PROTESTS

Charter Day festivities moved from the outdoor arena of the Illumination to the indoor venue of the lecture hall. A speech and presentation by a Massachusetts state senator who was also an alumna culminated the activities of the ritual. Students who were gathered in the auditorium buzzed about old and new Charter Days as well as judgments about the senator's controversial political views. A flier, circulated prior to the address, challenged the senator's stand on aid to pregnant mothers and women's rights. The Mount Holyoke norm of challenge and debate was dramatized during the senator's speech. Part of being a student at this college meant that you were concerned with activism and the critical thinking skills that such action cultivated. The *Student Handbook* contained written clarification of the policy on public dissent: the "College aims to provide an environment hospitable to open interchange of knowledge and opinion in terms of reasoned discourse. The citizen's right to free speech, free movement, free association, peaceful assembly, and orderly protest extend to every member of the college." The dean of students, sensing the confrontational mood among those lined across the back of the auditorium, used her introduction to restate the college's commitment to issues of debate and discussion: "A guiding principle of Mount Holyoke's life as a college has been a commitment to freedom of inquiry and expression and the right—and the responsibility—to disagree when that seems the appropriate response." Chuckling, the protesting students noted her acknowledgment of their demonstration.

A single page of scribbled notes betrayed a lack of preparation by the senator. The audience grew bored and restless as she rambled through unrelated and disconnected topics. Impatience turned to anger during the question-and-answer session as the senator failed to rise to the challenging questions presented by the students. After several failed attempts at an exchange, the senator retired from the podium.

CHARTER DAY MESSAGES

Rituals are often composed of several related activities. In the case of Charter Day, the tradition entailed a dinner identified with the college's history, the Illumination, and a speech. Each segment was an opportunity to communicate ritual messages and meanings to the college community. The discussion below summarizes some of those meanings including the contradictions conveyed through Charter Day, invention and danger, symbolic representations, intact mission, and a "total sense of history."

Contradictions

The senator's hasty exit after her speech emphasized a number of contradictions present during Charter Day.

(a) The genteel nature of the questionably named Gracious Dining was juxtaposed against the less-than-gracious confrontation aimed at the speaker.

(b) An established state leader was challenged by the emerging leaders among the students.

(c) Cynical response of the charter's arrival by horseback was set against the obvious pride students had for their institution.

(d) Despite the sentiments about the "stupidity" of Charter Day and "irrelevance" of Gracious Dining, students complied with the Sesquicentennial Committee's suggestion and stood at 6:15 p.m. to sing the alma mater. Cynicism gave way to tradition.

Risk, challenge, protest, and cynicism were part of a Mount Holyoke education. The push and pull evident in the debated ideas built a time-honored resilience and commitment to the ideals and principles of Mary Lyon's founding values.

Invention and Danger

An air of invention and danger pervaded this redesigned Charter Day performance. In keeping with the anthropological image of ritual and human living as rehearsal, the actions, messages, and symbols of Charter Day could have seriously backfired. The senator's speech, meant to inspire, did not come off as planned.

Respondents, particularly the Sesquicentennial Committee student chair, confessed in advance her doubts about whether the event would happen as planned. A performance's boundaries and participants' behavior are always characterized by danger and uncertainty.

Although more obvious and at risk during a first-time or redefined event, danger and uncertainty are present at all rituals. Anyone could, at any time, speak out of turn, refuse to follow the conforming actions of the leaders, or behave individually rather than collectively. But, participants usually accept the ritual-prescribed roles of follower and audience. They read from the script, listen attentively, and take their lead from those in charge. The behavior of the students who challenged the state senator was an anomaly among the ritual behavior observed. Challenge by the students was bounded by a set of rules about when and how it could occur: articulated in the classroom, expressed through student governance structures, and voiced during dormitory discussions.

Symbolic Representations

This particular Sesquicentennial Charter Day reenactment was unique among other rituals because the planners used symbols in an expanded way. These symbols included a horse, period dress, candles, time, and food. They helped vividly retell the story of the seminary's transformation into a college. Electric lights symbolized the candles of the first Illumination; a rolled piece of paper represented the original charter; a professor on horseback portrayed the original charter bearer. The building of the first Illumination, which burned to the ground in one of Mount Holyoke's many fires, was represented by another standing on the same site.

Symbols were used to communicate the college's founding ideals throughout the campus: building names, architecture, portraits, furnishings, program statements, plaques, speeches, and lecture introductions. Charter Day was another occasion to use symbols as statements about the college's ways of being. For example, the "genteel" traditions of an earlier age were retained through Gracious Dining. The visiting senator's speech became an opportunity to restate the college's ideals of challenge and egalitarianism. Time and its passage were used to restate the story of the college's founding. The Sesquicentennial Committee scheduled the expanded ritual on the anniversary of the original charter's arrival. The alma mater was sung in timed unison across campus to mark the charter's arrival. Charter Day, a normally minor tradition, became a stage upon which to restate, legitimate, and transform the college's culture.

To avoid a misunderstanding of the symbols, the story of the original charter was shared in advance as part of the event's publicity. Library and dining room table displays served as media through which to share history and convey meaning. The history of Mary Lyon's original intentions for the college was printed and circulated. Her vision for women's higher education and statements about the students' responsibility to perpetuate those ideals were shared as part of the ritual. This information not only shaped knowledge concerning the charter and the college's founding, the knowledge created meaning upon which the college's culture was perpetuated, shaped, and transformed. At the very least, the advance work created excitement for a heretofore minor ritual.

Intact Mission

During Charter Day at Mount Holyoke, Mary Lyon's founding intentions were not to be minimized. The mission she forged for the college was a vision to provide the highest quality higher education for women. The spirit of her one hundred and fifty-year-old vision was intact, dynamic, and adaptable. The secretary of the college, a non-alumna respondent, felt that for outsiders who had not seen the expression of this spirit, it was "hard to articulate a sense of what women's education can be."

The ideals and traditions upon which Mount Holyoke was founded were translated from the founder's words into the intentions of the modern college. These founding beliefs were the literal source of the ritual content. Ritual wording was often lifted verbatim from Mary Lyon's written documents. Her ideals (service, community, achievement, and social justice) so permeated the college's formal and informal rituals and structures that college members often conveyed her ideals as ones to which they personally ascribed. Respondents for this research repeatedly evoked the founder's original words to express their roles as students, alumnae, and administrators. Mary Lyon's words served as the content for college community ideas about the role of women's higher education.

Through rituals such as Charter Day, original and contemporary college ideals shaped one another in a dynamic interplay. The founding ideals would be meaningless without the diligent perpetuation of their meaning through the college culture. Likewise, the current use of these founding ideals as ritual content would be meaningless and hollow but for the strength of Mary Lyon's thoughts and convictions.

A "Total Sense of History"

The events of Charter Day added to what a senior respondent referred to as the college's "total sense of history." If the college was to endure, it needed caretakers of that history. Charter Day and other similar rituals embodied the message conveyed by this senior respondent that "this place continues." History repeated itself through the Illumination, horseback-delivered charter, Gracious Dining, and oft-sung alma mater. Mount Holyoke's past was chronicled through term papers, scripts, and cultural artifacts that students and others donated to the college's archives, a repository of living history.

When used as the content for rituals like Charter Day, the founding ideals remained at the heart of the college's purpose. As participants in the college's mission, community members perpetuated and strengthened a vibrant interplay between past and present. The ideals became visible through the creation of living history and enactment of those in ritual. The symbols and actions of the event celebrating the chartering of one of the first institutions for women's higher education spoke to the community members' pride about and understanding of the vision of women's higher education.

Charter Day was one event among many at Mount Holyoke that cultivated a fusion of institutional and individual histories. Despite this complex, information-laden society, the expense and effort expended on a ritual reaching back in history to a simpler time indicated the importance of the college's founding and its mission. Despite the information explosion communicated in the classroom and the challenges facing these future career women, scholars, and mothers, there were old, established "truths" to be spoken. These "truths" spoke to their place in the world as well as their connection to tradition and history.

CONCLUSIONS

Charter Day created, through its use of time, symbols, and space, an image of possibilities. People who exist in communities such as colleges thirst to embrace a vision beyond their individual thoughts and dreams. Through rituals, students and others can imagine a reality toward which they can aspire. Mount Holyoke's difficult yet successful founding and its enactment during Charter Day conveyed the message that anything was possible. The deeds of past heroines and the stories told about their feats reflect the courage and stamina permeating the very woodwork of the college. Viewed in the light of the women who preceded them, students realized that they could achieve anything. They shared a history and tradition of heroines.

Chapter 5

Secular Ceremony: Action, Order, and Evocation

> Ritual can be seen as an especially dramatic attempt to bring some particular part of life firmly and definitely into orderly control (Moore & Myerhoff, 1977, p. 3).

When Barbara Myerhoff published her research on a Jewish Senior Citizens home in 1978, ritual studies was a well-established field of anthropological study. Myerhoff had broken with the practice of studying the "other" and turned her interpretive lens on American culture. Myerhoff and her collaborator, Sally Moore (Moore & Myerhoff, 1977) coined the term "secular ceremony" for rituals enacted in Western societies. "Secular ceremonies are common in industrial societies and are found in all contexts . . . Meetings, covert trials, installations, graduations, and other formal assemblies of many kinds are part of the ordinary fabric of collective social life" (p. 4). This term emphasized the change from ritual as the expression of universals and religious beliefs to ritual as the communication of beliefs and attitudes within a secular nonreligious social context.

ANTHROPOLOGY OF EXPERIENCE

Sally Moore and Barbara Myerhoff advanced an anthropological perspective called the anthropology of experience (Bruner, 1986; Clifford & Marcus 1986; Geertz, 1988; Kapferer, 1986; Turner,V., 1984; Turner & Turner, 1985). This subdiscipline of anthropology emphasizes contextual meaning, complexity, indeterminacy, and uncertainty. In a postmodern tradition, ethnographies and case studies cannot tell the "truth" about a culture. They do not, "even in a vague way, invariably attach to a total explanation" (Moore & Myerhoff, 1977, p. 12). Rather, all understandings of the truth are partial—true only in a time-bound, contextual manner. This aspect conveys an interpretive quality on anthropological understanding and gives interpretations of cultural aspects such as rituals and traditions the ability to skirt the real and unreal. Secular ceremonies create an opportunity to define reality for that particular context in that particular time.

College and university administrators and faculty could not have invented a more apt form than secular ceremony to communicate the values and ideals of higher education. Since this cultural action "is a good form for conveying a message as if it were unquestionable, it often is used to communicate those very things which are most in doubt" (Moore & Myerhoff, 1977, p. 24). Higher education embraces some suspect purposes within democratic, ostensibly nonelitist American society. These include difficult to visualize, debatable ideals as pursuit of the life of the mind and intellectualism. What does an educated person look like? What is actually gained with a higher education degree? Why should the multiple, often conflicting, purposes of higher education be sanctioned? Why should the public good be invested in this selective system?

One can speculate that secular ceremony and other traditional practices such as ritual can be used to address these questions that have no adequate answers. They convince us of truths that are doubtful. Secular ceremony can present imperceptible values more objectively in such a way that they become more believable, less questioned, and more resistant to modification. Because synchronized, unified ritual action is out of the ordinary, its messages can convey meanings beyond the ordinary. In this way, secular ceremonies stabilize culture. This stabilization can often occur most aptly through creation of new beliefs. Cultural vitality can be better renewed through statements of new cultural values than maintenance of the original ones (Turner, V., 1974).

PROPERTIES OF SECULAR CEREMONIES

Myerhoff defined secular ceremony "as an act or actions intentionally conducted by a group of people employing one or more symbols in a repetitive, formal, precise, highly stylized fashion" (1977, p. 199). The stylized, repeated action of these events takes place in familiar forms easily recognized by participants and spectators. The properties of secular ceremonies (Moore & Myerhoff, 1977) were defined as follows:

(a) repetition in content, form, and occasion;
(b) self-conscious or deliberate action by the participant as part of the distinct behavior or stylized performance;
(c) orderly, stylized action achieved through exaggerated precision, extraordinary actions, or ordinary actions dramatized in unusual ways;
(d) evocative style, presentation, and staging to engage and focus the audience's attention;
(e) a collective dimension expressed in the ritual's message of community social meaning.

Many of the rituals and traditions (founder's days, charter days, award ceremonies) occurring on college campuses can be classified as secular ceremonies. They predominantly eschew religious association, reflect local rather than universal themes, and reinforce values specific to the college in which the ceremony is enacted. Unlike natural- and universal-oriented rituals such as fertility rites, secular ceremonies influence human, everyday reality.

Collective Dimension

Whether or not campus community members gather for the secular ceremonies offered on campus, all are invited. One of their purposes is to encourage the community to gather, at least for the duration of the ritual, as one. The collective nature of secular ceremony reveals a profound human need to form and live in communities. Rituals and ceremonies present opportunities for people to gather and verbalize the beliefs and values of community living. The fact that ceremonial participants recite words in unison and perform actions en masse significantly adds to the collective experience of secular ceremony.

College campuses, filled with diverse populations, stakeholders, and interest groups, must purposely strive to build unified communities. The collective action of secular ceremony achieves this purpose by gathering the various campus groups together, addressing truths all can at least partially accept, and creating a unity through simultaneously spoken messages and synchronized actions.

Choir singing and orchestral music during ceremonies has a particularly incorporating effect. Music such as a brass quartet during commencement, a glee club during baccalaureate, or an organ during a memorial service creates unifying, coordinating tempo (Rappaport, 1992). This tempo can be particularly dynamic during processionals and recessionals when participants are moving as one into and out of the ritual space.

Repetition

Graduations, inaugurations, and convocations have been part of ceremonial life on campus for well over three hundred years. Secular ceremonies within higher education began with the founding of Harvard College in 1636. Old and new campuses now employ ceremonial forms to build community as well as credibility. The use of ceremonies establishes that each campus, regardless of age, is part of the whole higher education enterprise. In this way, repetition of ceremonial form and content perpetuates old forms and provides a template upon which new forms are constructed.

Similar to the repetition of particular ceremonial forms, the campus cultural calendar is reproduced season to season, year to year. Repetition builds cultural predictability and stability (Myerhoff, 1984). As the academic year progresses, students and other community members anticipate rituals as a form promoting continuity of action and ideas.

On college campuses, whether or not student attendance warrants the attention and effort paid to particular events, specific rituals occur annually. While it is easy to see how repetition of time, place, and manner creates cultural stability, repetition also suggests cultural change.

No repetition is flawless: repetition can result in "culture lag and loss of meaning" (Goody, 1977, p. 30). Time lags, "faulty" reproduction, and the introduction of a new rendition builds modification and eventual cultural change. While form and content may resemble past performances, slight changes are always present. Unintentional faux pas, mistakes, and playfulness combine with intentional change of meaning and content. Therefore, secular ceremonies, unlike the stable, unadaptable form suggested in rites of passage theory, exist as a dynamic form that changes as much as it remains the same. Meaning is lost while new meaning is adopted.

Self-Conscious, Deliberate Action

Secular ceremonies contain language, action, and symbols unlike daily discourse and behavior. This out of the ordinary and stylized action gives ceremonies their convincing quality. "By high stylization and extraordinary uses—of objects, language, dress, gestures, and the like—ritual calls attention to itself, so that we cannot fail to see that its contents are set apart from ordinary affairs" (Myerhoff, 1984, p. 152). Accustomed from birth to the presence of rituals and ceremonies, humans easily recognize the stylized language and action. These endow the event with meaning drawn from the culture's belief system. People are taught through education and socialization what to expect during rituals. They know how the action is structured, what movements and responses are suggested, and the character of the messages conveyed. When they arrive in a ritual circumstance—even situations that are new—they still know how to act. This knowledge, often at a tacit level (Polanyi, 1983), feels fated or magical. In actuality, the knowledge about ritual practice is embedded so deep within their bodies and minds that they have no comprehension that it is there.

The importance of secular ceremony should not be underestimated. Similar to rites of passage, ceremonies are not merely a reflection of culture; they construct culture (McLaren, 1986).

A ceremony such as Founder's Day at Mount Holyoke College would first appear to have confusing, nonsensical language and actions. A centerpiece of the event occurs at dawn on the grave of Mary Lyon, the founder. At sunrise, the trustees serve ice cream to students within the wrought iron fence of the centrally located grave site. What meaning could such odd behaviors possibly have? And why at sunrise? Institutional history shows that during the early enactments of the event, ice cream was a rare treat. The flavor of the dessert was announced at daybreak by smoke emitted from the campus's heating plant. White for vanilla and black for chocolate divulged the limited choice. Only during ceremony could trustees be prevailed upon to forego their formal business demeanor and serve ice cream at the crack of dawn. Such actions reveal the belief in service to the students and the college as well as the sense of humor in which ceremonies are often enacted. No campus can take itself too seriously when ceremony is so playfully, and eccentrically, enacted (Manning, 1989a).

The stylization and contrived action of secular ceremony differs from everyday social life that is also routine, regular, and repetitive. Secular ceremonies, unlike the routines of daily living, are sporadic and unusual. A daily dose of secular ceremony would be too casual, decreasing the ceremony's ability to evoke emotions. In fact, the most important rituals are performed least often (Turner, V., 1977a).

Orderly Action

During secular ceremonies, people stand and sit in unison, synchronize their movements with other participants, and move in an orderly fashion. During commencement ceremonies, graduates process into the site, stand row by row to receive their diplomas, march across a stage, and simultaneously move their tassels from one side of their mortarboard to the other. Marshals and other ceremonial participants, often with great seriousness, use precise gestures to convey their intentions. These orderly actions endow the ceremony with meaning and significance.

Many of the actions performed during ceremonies are well known to participants, even if some of the graduates have never attended a commencement. Cues (e.g., gestures by marshals) enable the ceremony to proceed with a minimum of disorder and chaos. Such a minimally interrogative stance "is attention-commanding and deflects questioning at the same time" (Moore & Myerhoff, 1977, p. 8).

Evocative Presentation Style

Secular ceremonies are occasions during which people are moved to tears, laughter, and joyousness. Public displays of strong emotions are not only expected but are a sign that the ceremony is working. Secular ceremonies evoke emotions as a result of their actions and produce an attentive state of mind (Moore & Myerhoff, 1977). Music, stylized language, and symbols urge strong feelings and emotions. Creativity is invoked and commitment prescribed as a result of the emotional attachment built. Extraordinary language further adds to the evocative presentation style. Unusual substitutes for everyday language establish a commitment to values and beliefs not typically articulated in daily vernacular.

The actions, language, and messages of secular ceremonies and rituals must be convincing. Linking strong emotions to the suspect beliefs assures commitment and dedication. A ceremony that does not convince the community of immutable truths is dangerous to the health of the culture. Espousing ideologies, belief systems, and founding ideals, the very heart of what people believe about themselves, is serious business. If a college unconvincingly speaks to the "truth" of academic excellence, students will be hard-pressed to believe in themselves and their abilities. If faculty over-exaggerate their scholarship and research capabilities, the reputation of the institution is suspect. Ceremonies create disappointment if the messages expressed are too pretentious to be believed. Paradoxically, a ceremony's capacity to create meaning can convince people of seemingly implausible truths. With their dynamic form and evocative style, ceremonies convey messages convincing participants that their loftiest dreams and most outrageous aspirations are possible.

DYNAMICS WITHIN SECULAR CEREMONIES

The form of secular ceremonies including repetition, self-conscious action, stylization, evocative presentation, and collective dimension facilitates a variety of cultural dynamics (Moore & Myerhoff, 1977). Of these, multivocality, reflexivity, and form and meaning making have particular significance within higher education.

Multivocality

Secular ceremonies and the actions, language, and symbols contained within them offer opportunities for many voices to be expressed and heard.

> At each successive moment during a ritual's performance an array of varied significata may be *concurrently* represented to participants by single objects or acts. Conversely, a single significatum may be *concurrently* represented by a plethora of *simultaneously* performed acts or perceived objects (Rappaport, 1992, p. 8).

Symbols, language, and ceremonial action are susceptible to many meanings but usually possess and/or evoke a core meaning linked to the central problems of the age (Turner, V., 1974). In higher education these issues include the vocational emphasis of students, lack of public trust, financial exigencies, conflicts over cultural diversity, and exorbitant tuition costs (Lenington, 1996; Levine, 1997). Ceremonies speak to these issues by incorporating them into the themes of rituals. The multivocal quality of the ceremonies enacts creative solutions and previously ignored possibilities.

Multivocality occurs as spectators and participants interpret the messages of the ceremony against the context of their personal experience. But these symbols, actions, and language of ceremonies are not linked to universal, uniformly interpreted beliefs as in rites of passage. Instead, people interpret numerous meanings from a single ceremonial symbol.

Because of the multivocality of symbols and language, profound disagreement about the meaning and substance of secular ceremonies is possible as various messages are produced and interpreted. From a postmodern perspective, there is no one absolute way to interpret the messages generated through rituals and secular ceremonies. While the form may have some common characteristics, the interpretation of that form and the actions composing them are highly individualized and speculative.

Multivocality, through its ability to engender multiple meanings, creates dynamism. The multiple interpretations combine with the inexact replication of ceremonies to create a vigorous, uncertain form. While cultural boundaries certainly exist, almost anything is possible. In fact, given the obvious multiple interpretations of ceremonial action, symbols, and language, it is surprising that any consensus about cultural meaning is achieved at all.

An example of the multivocal and dynamic quality of ceremonies can be seen in the interpretations of a speech delivered at a ritual. Reviews and interpretations can range from boring to inspiring and everything in between. Each listener can reflexively fold the words into his or her experiences to form a personal interpretation. While one person may find nothing at all in his or her personal history to connect with the speaker's words, another may find that they strike a chord and inspire insights not previously imagined.

Reflexivity

Reflexivity, a uniquely human capability, is the "capacity of human beings to distance themselves from their own subjective experiences, to stand apart from and to comment on them" (MacAloon, 1984, p. 11). The extraordinary time and place created for the ceremony bring about an interruption in daily living. Space is fashioned in which reflection can occur and questions be raised. Actions can be viewed from new perspectives; regrets as well as triumphs can be reviewed and evaluated. Without the interruption created during ceremony, much of life would progress without reflection. There simply would not be any time, especially in Western culture with the value it places on constant activity, to reflexively consider one's life.

Humans can examine their actions, assess the underlying drives compelling them to act, and change subsequent actions based on reflexive action. Reflexivity is essentially acting with understanding and awareness. Reflexive action enables the cultural participant to see his or her current actions, feelings, and thoughts in the context of the past and future. Folding the past into the present in anticipation of the future brings about growth and development.

Secular ceremonies, similar to rites of passage (see chapter 3) and cultural performances (see chapter 9), are rich opportunities for reflexive action. Reflexive action through secular ceremonies can occur on two levels: individual and cultural.

Individual Reflexivity. During a secular ceremony, participants are able to stand back and examine their lives objectively. When individuals attend a ceremony, they encounter messages and actions. Experiencing the emotions evoked through the ceremony, they are able "to objectify their action and experience in the context of the rite, and to stand back or distance themselves from their action within the rite so they can reflect upon their own and others' actions and understandings" (Kapferer, 1984, p. 180). In addition to reflecting on his or her life as an expression of the person he or she chooses to be, reflexivity allows the individual to place his or her actions, thoughts, and feelings in a larger cultural context. The ceremonial participant is not a solitary member of the culture. Rather, his or her life has significance in the larger social context.

Higher education and the achievement of a degree is predominantly a private affair. The primary activities involved depend on solitude (e.g., reading and writing) and individual achievement. During higher education ceremonies, the private becomes public in dramatic ways. This switch of the private to public is so commonplace that it does not provoke discomfort to have one's academic accomplishments paraded out in front of an audience. This private to public switch is unthinkable, even associated with negative behaviors such as bragging, in non-ritualized settings. Ritual is a potent cultural form for the transformation of the sacred or private to the profane or public.

Human beings as reflexive creatures are aware of the underlying assumptions of their actions, behaviors, and feelings. They not only can express their feelings, thoughts, and actions but can reflect on the origins of those human attributes. No other creature has this reflexive capacity.

Cultural Reflexivity. Meaning, during a ritual or secular ceremony, is not the private domain of the individual subjects, spectators, or performers. During ceremony, individual meaning fuses with group meaning and vice versa to create culture. In many ways, ceremonies are a cultural lightning rod for creating meaning. Through their form as well as their ability to intensely focus attention and action, ceremonies provoke and symbolize meaning.

Ceremonies speak to meaning that grows out of or is folded back into the culture. Whether one agrees or disagrees with the enactment or messages, ceremonies affect the community. Public and private beliefs are open to examination and influence. Through a shared display of meaning, evocative symbols, and actions, ceremonies are a powerful expression of culture.

Rituals and ceremonies on college campuses are potent reminders of humankind's drive to create meaning within cultural settings. With meaning as an "essential element of human existence" (Orphanides, 1992, p. 109), it comes as no surprise that these ceremonies address identity, community, commitment, purpose, achievement, growth, and leadership, among other issues. These aspects of human living are not usually discussed, nor are they taken for granted. In many ways, they are too important to risk being treated casually. The formality, stylization, and evocative emotions of ceremonies signal their importance as well as creating a time and place to reflect upon them.

Honors ceremonies employ ethical and moral rhetoric to clarify significant achievements. Convocations direct the community's attention to the most worthy attributes of their members. Alumni gatherings entreat community members to picture their actions in the larger, cultural context. Honor society initiations encourage participants to undertake challenges previously avoided. In each, the message expressed is that a person's identity and actions have significance beyond his or her private existence. Each person is part of the whole. Individual actions become cultural capital, and cultural capital is used to achieve individual ambitions (Bourdieu, 1977). The formation of campus communities, achievement of college leaders, and perpetuation of campus cultures could not exist without the meaning-making actions of ceremonies and other cultural expressions.

Meaning making through ceremonial action is no small task on college campuses. These institutions inherited the societal responsibility of intellectual, physical, spiritual, and emotional growth (American Council on Education, 1937; 1949). While significant aspects of students' identities are established prior to college attendance, integrity, justice, and compassion are a sampling of values that can be significantly enhanced during the college years. Ceremony's capacity to evoke sentiment and emotion creates an opportunity to address issues normally avoided. Convocations with the theme of social justice can confront intolerance. Graduation speakers can implore students and their family members to seek success beyond materialism. Honorary degree recipients can act as role models of integrity. "The efficacy of ritual to effect transformations of experience and identity, and to provide participants with deeper insights into the nature of their cultural and social life, depends on the ritual performance generating conditions for reflexive action" (Kapferer, 1984, p. 188).

Through the cultural shaping quality of higher education ceremonies, the following questions can be considered: Are our purposes, as visually expressed in the ceremony, congruent with our behaviors? Do we really do what we claim? Are there places where our achievements fall short of our aspirations? Does higher education achieve the moral and social purposes requested by society? Campuses often use national and international events as a source of meaning for their ceremonies. The Persian Gulf War sparked vigils; commemoration services mark national crises. Even a simple gesture such as a flag lowered to half staff has significant cultural meaning. Without these traditions, the campus culture would be endowed with less meaning.

Meanings as expressed through secular ceremony are linked to the culture's ideology. Cultural reproduction and ideological creation are promoted within cultures through traditional cultural mechanisms such as secular ceremony. Critical theorists in educational theory focus on the reproduction side of this dynamic to discuss how educational institutions reproduce ideological systems not necessarily in the best interest of the students. Similar to the structural anthropologists, these theorists view cultural activities such as ritual and ceremony as reproducing underlying ideologies of paternalism, capitalism, and bureaucracy. While these theorists are criticized as being overly deterministic (relying on universal forces divorced from human action), nonhistorical, narrow, and extreme (Ellsworth, 1989; Ortner, 1984), their approach can assist one to understand the cultural mechanisms at play within higher education.

Higher education has been criticized as mindlessly reproducing the middle class, stripping participants of their critical thinking ability, and focusing on the materialism of capitalism (hooks, 1994). Further indictments about the tenets underlying higher education include racist ideology and practices. Whether one agrees or disagrees with these accusations, it is clear that cultural events such as ceremonies deliver powerful messages to spectators and participants. When combined with the potential for danger and multivocality, ceremonies can act as forceful mechanisms for cultural change and permanence. The question is what change is occurring, based on what beliefs, and with what consequences.

While the critical theorists' interpretation of the power of ceremonies and other cultural forms is compelling, it is clear that the forms and actions of secular ceremonies "need not be 'attached' to a worked-out, elaborate ideology" (Moore & Myerhoff, 1977, p. 10). Secular ceremonies are most effective in building commitment, reinforcing community, and encouraging identity through their persuasive form rather than through their ideological attachment. In ceremony, it seems that persuasion is more effective when the message is subtly delivered through consistent and multiple symbolism. This situation is particularly the case in higher education where ideologies are often numerous and indiscernible (Birnbaum, 1991). In a setting where multiple goals and disparate purposes abound, secular ceremonies create the impression of stability, communion, and singularity of mission.

FORM AND MEANING MAKING

Secular ceremonies are intimately related to human meaning-making activities.

Their dual capability to express existing cultural meaning while simultaneously creating new meaning demonstrates "mankind's [sic] undying insistence in stating not only that life has meaning but also specifying what that meaning is" (Myerhoff, 1977, p. 218).

The form of secular ceremony (location, process, history) is as essential to the communication of meaning as the words spoken and the messages expressed. One can see "movement as much as structure, persistence as much as change, indeed, persistence as a striking aspect of change" (Turner, V., 1974, p. 32).

Baccalaureate and other ceremonies performed in the Mount Holyoke College chapel relied on the preexisting form of Protestant ceremonies previously enacted in that space. The existing ceremonial form lent structure and significance to the newer renditions. The chapel, in fact, could not be sacred ritual space without those former ceremonies. This reality caused justifiable consternation for Jewish and international students who found the Christian-based ceremonies unwelcoming (Manning, 1989a). Despite the secular nature of the college, the ceremonies were deeply rooted in a religious past. The chapel's architecture and religious symbolism as well as campus storytelling of past mandatory chapel attendance let the students know that even the most nonreligious ceremonies rested on a sacred form. Time, place, and practice combined in the ceremony to create a form that clearly communicated multiple meanings.

But, this secular ceremony form differs substantially from its rites of passage forerunner. The structure of ceremony does not adhere to a universal form. Ceremonial form looks more like a rehearsal than formal performance in the ways it yields to the purposes of the event, molds its form to the specific cultural context, and accommodates itself to the whims of the participants. All of the intentions and effects of secular ceremonies are indeterminate and open to interpretation by spectators and performers (Moore & Myerhoff, 1977). Form and content are reorganized and rearranged to fit particular purposes rather than universal ideals.

SUMMARY

Moore and Myerhoff's (1977; Myerhoff, 1977; 1978; 1984) concepts about secular ceremony provide a framework with which to understand the mutually shaping nature of rituals and cultural meaning. "Above all rituals are dramas of persuasion. They are didactic, enacted pronouncements concerning the meaning of an occasion, and the nature and worth of the people involved" (Myerhoff, 1977, p. 222). Understanding the properties of secular ceremonies can help participants speculate on the way these events simultaneously perpetuate and create cultural beliefs through the meaning-making opportunity of form and action.

Chapter 6

Second Semester Convocation

"When I heard the music . . . I thought that they would have Latin and it would be boring."
—Convocation participant

Seniors dressed in their black regalia without the traditional academic hoods crowded into the lobby of the administration building. This spring semester they were the guests of honor at their final convocation. Excitement and anticipation filled the crowded hallway as students laughed, called out to their classmates, and huddled affectionately against one another. All members of the Mount Holyoke College community were encouraged to attend Convocation though new students and seniors were the primary participants.

The faculty, gathering before the ritual in the crowded basement of the same building, could hear the seniors overhead. They, too, laughed and greeted each other after the long semester break. In contrast to the seniors's garb, the black, scarlet, and gold of their robes was punctuated with academic hoods signifying institution, degree, and field of study. The faculty present were said to be the most committed of their ranks, part of a self-selected crowd who attended the twice-yearly Convocations to offer friendship and support to the students. Convocations at the beginning of each semester opened the term and welcomed new students into the Mount Holyoke community. In addition to its welcoming function, Second Semester Convocation honored outstanding leaders among upper class students. The faculty's presence on this rainy, cold winter evening signified their commitment.

Second Semester Convocation was vastly different from the fall semester celebration held six months earlier. Fall Semester Convocation was held in an outdoor amphitheater amidst the merrymaking of returning and new students. During Fall Semester Convocation seniors were adorned with their newly acquired caps and gowns for the first time. The Convocation was the first of many occasions during which they would wear their regalia. Unlike most colleges where seniors wore regalia only during Commencement, the culminating college ritual, Mount Holyoke seniors wore regalia often during their final college semesters. The end-of-the-summer heat during Fall Convocation pressured many to wear shorts and

T-shirts underneath their austere robes. The academically oriented Fall Convocation was made fun of, reversed and appropriated by the students to make it their own. Hair dyed class-color blue reflected college pride and the touch of craziness encouraged among the students at Mount Holyoke.

In contrast to outdoor informality of Fall Convocation, Second Semester Convocation occurred in the formal confines of the college chapel. Dignified and proper, the script and score were carefully selected by the planning committee to reflect Mount Holyoke's founding beliefs. During this particular convocation, the stage was set to acknowledge Mount Holyoke's diversity. This goal was congruent with the institution's founding goals to educate women who had been without access to higher education. Diversity, at least economically, was assured among the college's first students through the financial support available to women of varying economic backgrounds. Designed to be affordable to the daughters of farmers and merchants as well as the rich, Mount Holyoke had drawn a wide diversity of women from its earliest days.

This convocation ritual created time and space for the community to gather and celebrate their community of diverse people. From the pulpit high above the pews, the dean of the college chapel explained that Second Semester Convocation was a time for "corporate statements."

While faculty and administration were "transformed by the privilege" of attending Second Semester Convocation, a senior respondent declared that many seniors were relieved that "it's the last convocation they have to go to." Her class was counting down to graduation. The dwindling time, in her opinion, was a welcome relief as they changed from students to educated women. Convocation was an affirmation of their past and a harbinger of their future. Freshmen, in contrast, were hearing the first of many speeches espousing the image of who they could be as students and individuals. These rituals, as described by a non-alumna administrator, were "a punctuation in a person's life."

The faculty assumed their honored position at the front of the convocation procession. A faculty member designated as the marshal led the double line of marchers to the accompaniment of organ music. The dean of the college chapel credited Mount Holyoke's reputation for doing "such a good job on ceremony" to the participants' willingness to be led. She said the fiercely independent academic community was "willing to be told what to do during a ceremony" for the sake of the community.

Word had spread among students and faculty that this convocation ritual would be different from the past. The dean of the college chapel prayed from the pulpit that we are "gathered here before you of our own choosing . . . we seek to pursue our goals with honesty and respect." She was joined in the chancel by the president, dean of students, the Catholic chaplain, glee club, and honored guests.

A wide variety of the college's student cultures, diverse through the presence of international students, students of color, and women of different economic backgrounds, was represented. Racial incidents, on campus and at area schools (racial slurs written on a building, near-riot at a local university) encouraged the convocation planners to emphasize plurality. The concept jumped out from the first prayerful reading. Prayers of Hindu, Muslim, Jewish, and Christian faiths were sung, recited, spoken.

"Allah, lah, lah" reverberated through the chapel as Muslim students heard a public reading from the Koran and the words of Allah for perhaps the first time since they arrived at Mount Holyoke. The words traveled up to the balcony and echoed off the intricately painted organ pipes. The rose window glittered blue, red, and white in the subdued light of the chandeliers. Stained glass edged the side aisles and windowed transoms opened to the side chapel and entrance ways.

In the words of Mount Holyoke's president, the administration was committed to paying "attention to people who haven't been attended to before." The dean of the college chapel felt the planning committee was "disturbing the conventional." The ritual modeled diversity and extolled the virtues of difference. She felt rituals were a time when people "aren't embarrassed by emotions"; during ritual one can say "I care about this—it matters to me."

The use of ritual to approach sensitive issues of racism and diversity had roots in past practice. The planners employed a traditional and ceremonial form as a medium for a recently conceived, nationally imperative message. The adaptable, resilient form could bring content about difference into a public forum. Diversity, difference, and racism could be addressed within an emotional, not exclusively intellectual, realm. Ritual is an apt form because when it works, voltage and content come together. The "location, time, participants, and music all shape meaning whether you want it to or not . . . . Ceremonies carry content that discussions cannot," reflected the chapel dean.

As the ritual proceeded, syllables were barely audible as the sounds overlapped in the cavernous chapel. Female voices reciting phrases of the four religions resonated from the pulpit. The readings and chapel setting reinforced a religious, spiritual tone. The prayers, invocations, uncomfortable pews, echoing acoustics, and inspirational music embodied spirituality.

Struggling with Latin and Hebrew, the women prevailed through their faulty pronunciation. It was less important that the words be correctly pronounced than that the students offer their interpretation and "authentic voice." They had a right to recite the prayers of different religions and offer their interpretation rather than language proficiency.

Boundaries of difference were transcended to embrace interrelatedness. All women, regardless of belief, heard the words of religions different from their own. The convergence of different traditions reinforced the dean of student's comments that the college had a "commitment to broaden the multi-cultural community," accept other people's views, and be willing to discuss anything. The ritual publicly acknowledged the practice of encouraging students to shed their ethnocentrism. The minority and international students "want to look out and be affirmed." The majority culture women would get "a lesson in all these cultures."

The diversity espoused during Second Semester Convocation was an acrimonious issue for this college. Explicit statements valuing a diverse campus often provoked cynicism. A prominent criticism voiced by some students claimed that only those individual differences that did not stray from the middle-class, white norm were tolerated. Administrators and faculty challenged each student "to be all one could" but failed to fully acknowledge that the environment did not challenge or support all students equitably. The celebrated academic demands presented by the college were certainly a challenge for students of color and nontraditional students who juggled home ways with college ways, prejudice and discrimination, and uneven sources of support.

A Black alumna reflected that, "I didn't understand the preaching or songs that I heard in chapel when I was a student here." Second Semester Convocation, modeled on New England Christian services, was unfamiliar to women from urban America, Muslim backgrounds, or different regions of the United States. "It's because no one's talking to you—no one's saying 'welcome' to you." Women of color, in particular, were cautious about these rituals used in the past to exclude them from colleges and organizations.

Diversity and plurality were ironically set against the institutional objective of individual growth and achievement. Students of color struggled to be less isolated and to become part of the college community while simultaneously maintaining their cultural identity. These students were forced, in this paradox of community and individualism, to question their cultural identity while being challenged to their fullest as individuals. Mount Holyoke women were encouraged "to create a dream and the passion to pursue it; the ability to soar with that goal whether it be academic excellence, social justice, or service to others." But some students (Black, Hispanic, Asian and Native American) had to transcend barriers of prejudice and intolerance just to walk through the college's gates. With their identity as women of color confronted daily, they experienced personal challenges at many different levels. Despite this everyday reality, the many-leveled complexity of the diversity issue was merely hinted at during this Second Semester Convocation.

The glee club swayed as the conductor, a silver-haired woman, led the choir through "Alunde Alluya," an African prayer lullaby.

O, God of the sunrise,

Protect this child.

Help the infant to grow,

And become a worthy member of our tribe.

Her animated movements and exaggerated facial expressions spurred the glee club members to smile—and sing hard. Modulated harmonies were accompanied by the quiet dignity of a single drum. Sounds of Africa contrasted sharply with the churchlike organ music of the processional.

This year's Convocation intermingled music slightly out of place (African drums in a New England-style chapel, Spanish lyrics sung by casually dressed musicians) to challenge the students to recognize difference. As queried in a letter to the student newspaper, "Is this not a liberal arts institution which prides itself on diversity and open mindedness?" The ritual would represent "that cultural potpourri that nourishes and inspires the uncommon woman."

The students listened with selective attentiveness; a buzz of conversation ebbed and flowed. But the murmur of voices diminished as Hispanic musicians moved to the center of the chancel. Two men and a woman, dressed in casual clothing, holding native instruments, positioned themselves in front of the regalia-clad audience.

As the performers sang, the mood of the crowd changed. Energy rippled through the audience. People sat straighter. The audience was more attentive. Side conversations stopped. Students, faculty, and guests smiled and woke up from the gentle lulling of prayers and speeches. Music and lyrics from Bolivia and Paraguay reverberated through the chapel, enlivening the audience though the meaning of the words may have been lost on the predominantly English-speaking audience. The lute and high-pitched instruments awoke emotions previously untapped during the ritual. Zealous clapping and cheering exploded at the conclusion of the song, and the trio appeared embarrassed at this enthusiastic response. The ritual's pinnacle was reached. Faces were enraptured, people applauded wildly, and cheering occurred at length.

A motion from the dean of students signaled the audience to rise. It was time to recognize student leaders who had unselfishly served the college community. As names were announced and citations read, the honored women approached the chancel." They have distinguished themselves with their efforts on behalf of their peers and our community." The ritual was an acknowledgment that there is something "very spiritual—something very special" about women's leadership.

The candid and at times humorous citations spurred the students on: "have enhanced the quality of student life," "endless meeting times," "not intimidated by faculty, administrators or whoever she was working with," "significant contribution to the life of Mount Holyoke," "frustrations and joy of leadership." Noisy expressions of pride and support emanated from the students who acknowledged their peers' achievements. Support reinforcing their belief in each other was obvious. "One of the things that we're about here is support systems for women."

The student leaders honored fulfilled multiple on- and off-campus leadership positions. These were not one-dimensional women; their leadership was accompanied by high academic achievement and lofty goals for future scholarship. A common message thread through the ritual: those honored could be any of us; they represent all of us.

The setting of Second Semester Convocation was conspicuously artificial, the language deliberately obtuse and formal, the dress far from everyday. The ritual was distinguished by an ever present possibility of failure; the words, music, and drama might not spark the emotion desired. Pre-ceremonial conversations among students expressed the sentiment that these rituals were "pretty silly." But despite this cynical approach, the language and symbols of the ritual stirred emotions: "It slowly envelopes you"; "All of a sudden you are in over your head."

Lift every voice and sing,

Sing a song full of faith that the dark past has taught us;

Sing a song full of the hope that the present has brought us;

Facing the rising sun of our new day begun.

The Black national anthem concluded the award granting ritual of Second Semester Convocation. The printed music and lyrics were largely ignored as students and faculty sang the anthem without accompaniment. Women's voices created an emotionally moving sound as the students, faculty, and participants sang in unison.

Seniors, families, and audience members remained in their seats while beaming faculty processed down the center aisle. Formality was finally broken as people poured out of the pews to find friends and family. "That African song was the best that they've sung . . ."

The success of the experiment in diversity was confirmed as administrators and students hugged, kissed, and offered their review of the speeches, readings, and music. Families not expected to be present at the ritual occupied the heart of the festivities. They joined in the efforts to offer support and honor the women's leadership.

Outside the rainy night had turned warm. Seniors filtered through the campus decked in their regalia. As they walked through the grove, their robes ballooned in the night air. Arm in arm with bodies and heads bent together the students formed a haunting silhouette in the light of oncoming cars. The trees in the grove and shadows of the buildings provided a beautiful backdrop for a night of ritual.

PATTERNS AND THEMES OF MEANING

Several patterns and themes emerged during the ritual and through its retelling in the case study above. These themes include community, individuality, and valuing individual difference.

Community

The theme of community, expressed primarily through speeches, prayers, and music, was clearly evident during Second Semester Convocation. This theme was communicated through participants' statements such as "many of us will serve," "express our collective gratitude and appreciation," what "we believe in." Each statement reinforced important aspects of the community and essential college goals. These included "interest, involvement, and service" to the college and the "ability to soar with that goal whether it be academic excellence, social justice, or service to others."

In addition to the sentiment communicated through the messages of Second Semester Convocation, collectiveness was reflected in likeness of dress, movement, and behavior. The seniors were attired in academic robes resembling the faculty's. The mutually shared academic goals of students and faculty were represented through these nearly identical academic robes. Professors, dressed in the trappings of their academic status, stood as symbols and examples of the educated rank toward which the students were progressing.

The emphasis on scholarship, represented in statements about the academic challenge and symbolized in dress, language, and behavior, built a community of scholars among the students. The community of women scholars image was deeply rooted in Mount Holyoke's history. From the institution's earliest days, Mary Lyon, its founder, and the people who followed her as president placed emphasis on homelike residence halls, comfortable serene settings conducive to intellectual discussion, and a collegial ideology stressing service and sacrifice for the good of the whole.

Mount Holyoke's tradition of service, community, and sacrifice as crafted at a time of homogenous student populations and less complex institutional structures. Today, with its growing cadre of international, first-generation, minority, and adult students, the message of community was more complex. The traditional rituals celebrating community were strange, foreign even, from students' ideas of communal living. Community, as traditionally stated, possessed an underlying assumption of similarity (shared values, backgrounds, and experiences). Inclusiveness has different implications for homogeneous as opposed to heterogeneous populations.

The message gaining momentum nationally and voiced during Second Semester Convocation was the need for higher education to change to be a more inclusive and welcoming community. In an effort to fulfill this commitment of valuing difference, the collective language, behavior, and symbolism of Second Semester Convocation was contrasted with the imperatives of diversity. The values of the community took on a multicultural hue as Latino music, minority student awards, and readings from four religions were used in an adapted form of the medieval ritual.

The revised message of community expressed during Second Semester Convocation included difference (heterogeneity) as well as similarity (homogeneity). Community was not dependent on agreement and similarity of perspective. Community in modern colleges and universities required an appreciation and celebration of difference as well as a recognition of similarity. In fact, the former approach can be argued to be a more robust community because differences and disparities are faced rather than glossed over or accepted without question.

Individuality

The Second Semester Convocation message of commonality and unity contradicted the equally strong founding ideal of individual achievement. The dean of the college chapel expressed the contradiction between individual and community goals most eloquently when she said that during ritual people abandoned their individual differences and "allowed themselves to be led." As individuals with strong identities, community members were willing to compromise and act in corporate ways during ritual in the name of community. They allowed themselves to immerse their identity into the communal identity. Ritual is a time for corporate statements and communal behavior.

For all of the statements about community and commonality, awards were presented according to a meritocratic and authoritative structure. The organizational form, lines of authority, and underlying structure of Second Semester Convocation were distinctly paternalistic as administrators determined who was granted awards. Achievements were measured against an established norm of progress rather than an individual's personally crafted merit. The formal authority of the administrators and faculty was symbolized by their forward place of honor and elevated status during the ritual. The meritocratic reward system that students would experience in future employment was strongly reinforced by the hierarchical system used to determine awards for the ritual. While service to the community was acknowledged and celebrated, individuals, not groups, were recognized as exerting leadership. Recognized and honored leadership, in this context, was more an individual act exercised *on* others, less a communal act exercised *with* others.

Valuing Individual Differences

While the meritocratic structure was firmly reflected in the reward structure, it was partially abandoned to deliberately value and recognize individual differences. Students from groups previously underrepresented in the student leadership structure were featured, recognized, and honored. Those administrators authorizing the award recipient choices remained flexible within the authoritarian reward structure to recognize students different from the norm. Rewards were given to students of color involved in community service and campus leadership.

Second Semester Convocation was a response to a nationwide challenge for colleges and universities to attend to students of color on their campuses (Fleming, 1984; Hawkins, 1989; Katz, 1989; Stage & Manning, 1992). "As these minority groups become more actively recruited to higher education, institutions will be under pressure to respond to the different learning styles, diverse social and emotional needs, and educational expectations of many of these new participants" (Garland, 1985, pp. 12-13).

The changes—and tensions—accompanying a shift in the student populations attending colleges and universities are evident on campuses. Racial incidents on campus dramatically increased during the 1980s (Collison, 1988). The federal government's de-emphasis on issues of equity and affirmative action between 1980 and 1988 encouraged decreased levels of financial aid. There was a sharp disparity between the need to maintain enrollments and meet the ethical challenges to serve *all* students (including students of color) in relation to the lack of campus readiness to adapt ways of operating and structures to different cultural behaviors and standards.

A respondent who had graduated in the Class of 1921 interpreted the actions and messages of Second Semester Convocation as a reflection of Mount Holyoke's increased diversity and complexity. America was more homogenous during her time as a student. The people who sent their daughters to Mount Holyoke were from similar Anglo-Saxon stock. She reflected that a common point of view was more difficult in a country now characterized by numerous major cultural groups and diverse perspectives.

College rituals were increasingly being used to extol the message of diversity and multiculturalism. In response to racial incidents at local colleges, the realities of the student body changes, and the diversity rallying cry read weekly in *The*

Chronicle of Higher Education and other higher education publications, the ritual planners incorporated this quintessential modern theme into its medieval ritual. As American society was becoming more diverse and fragmented, planners used ceremonial forms to restate the message of community in the face of an overwhelming diversity. Disparate segments of the campus community struggled to join together in a united, coherent effort. Old ritual structures re-stated a modern imperative.

CONCLUSIONS

Second Semester Convocation and its messages of community and diversity epitomized the struggle for racial and ethnic equality on college campuses and in American society. The distinction made on this campus about the diversity issue involved the long-established ideals of egalitarianism, social justice, and service. Mount Holyoke College was founded in 1837 to serve women not previously educated at the highest levels. The revolutionary idea was reflected in the current mission, reinterpreted in light of the increase in students of color and shifted national demographics. True egalitarianism among a community of equals meant restructuring the basic ideals, symbols, and rituals to represent, reshape, and transform college ideals.

The dynamics dramatized in Second Semester Convocation included egalitarian values and respect for diversity. These values, particularly as contrasted with the growing national racism and Mount Holyoke's history of moral purpose, were congruent with the founding ideals of the college. Through Second Semester Convocation and other dramatizations of the equality dialogue, the college was continually reinterpreting its mission in light of national imperatives.

Chapter 7

Structure, Communitas, and Liminality

> Communitas is a fact of everyone's experience . . . . It is, however, central to religion, literature, drama, and art, and its traces may be found deeply engraved in law, ethics, kinship, and even economics. It becomes visible in tribal rites of passage, in millenarian movements, in monasteries, in the counterculture, and on countless informal occasions (Turner, V., 1974, p. 231).

When one reads Victor Turner's writings on rituals, communitas, and structure, a rich interpretation of the possibilities of human action unfolds. Mining the untapped potential of van Gennep's liminality, Turner expanded ritual theory to encompass complex explanations of social living. He took crises and showed how growth and order ensue. He urged understanding of the purposes of the institutional and social system structures that pervade our lives. He linked the dynamism of social structures to cultural processes such as ritual. Turner's theory of rituals can assist one to understand that through the liminality, communitas, and anti-structure triggered by ritual, opportunities for the "free play of mankind's [sic] cognitive and imaginative capacities" are created (Turner & Turner, 1985, p. 161).

Turner defined ritual as "a transformative performance revealing major classifications, categories, and contradictions of cultural processes" (Turner & Turner, 1985, p. 171). Rituals, accordingly, have stereotyped sequences of activities, behavior, and language. They possess the extraordinary ability to create and transform the socially constructed structure and beliefs of communities (Bal, 1990). The depth and complexity of ritual action can be understood primarily in the context of humankind's most fundamental meaning-making activities. Rituals were, for Turner, no less than a mirror of humankind.

Through their playful, performative genre, rituals serve a variety of purposes. They criticize, subvert, uphold and modify behaviors, values, activities, and relationships. Rituals, as performances, resemble play or rehearsal, need an audience, contain plots and scores, and offer synchronized action. As collective events, they mirror cultural and social processes, roles, status, and behaviors (Turner & Turner, 1985). In fact, rituals disclose the most fundamental, imperative aspects of cultural meaning when they tell stories and make statements about the community's quality of life (Turner & Turner).

STRUCTURE AND ANTI-STRUCTURE

Victor Turner discussed two complementary modes of social life: structure and anti-structure. The latter concept he also called communitas. While structure explains the organization of roles, power, status, and property (Lewis, 1980), communitas is structureless. It represents the whole of humanity. Paradoxically sides of the same mirror, neither anti-structure and structure, could exist without the other. "Communitas has an existential quality; it involves the whole man in his relation to other whole men. Structure, on the other hand, has cognitive quality . . . it is essentially a set of classifications, a model for thinking about culture and nature and ordering one's public life" (Turner, V., 1969, p. 127). The characteristics of structure and anti-structure as well as the meaning making informing their formation is very evident during rituals. As the catalyst for communitas, rituals model practices dictated by structure, raise the questions imperative in human living, engender the emotion and commitment of liminality, and provide a way for anti-structure to become folded into structure. The rituals that define structure and anti-structure tend to occur at the edges or interstices of society, time, and place (Turner, V., 1974). These edges could be the beginning and end of the college years, when change threatens to disrupt the campus social structure, or when a ripple in history and time dictates reconsidered social roles.

Structure

All societies, to free themselves of chaos and ambiguity, create structure. Structure, associated with obligation, jurality, law, and constraint, is abstract. It demonstrates the social roles and status definitions of social systems. Structure has visible and invisible aspects. It can be readily identified in founding values and principles, legal codification, and belief structures. The bureaucratic necessities of institutional life are an excellent example of the abstract structure created by humankind. Social rules of manners and etiquette are expressions of structure. Structure is not easy to describe or discuss because it is learned tacitly; one adheres to the rules and practices of structure without thinking. People know from being socialized in a particular culture or social setting that certain behaviors are acceptable.

Higher education, using Turner's concepts of structure and anti-structure, emphasizes structure. Institutions of higher education and the educational system generally rigidly define roles (rank, administrative titles), behavior (bureaucratic procedures, disciplinary systems), power (rewards and punishments), status (degrees), and property (functional limits on physical space such as classrooms and dormitories).

Ritual is related to structure in the way that its emphasis on themes, processes, and stories allows participants to learn the values, rules, and behavior styles of a culture (Turner, V., 1977a). Rituals can make structural aspects such as sanctioned behaviors, hierarchy of authority, sexual opposition, principles, norms, and role allocation visible (Turner & Turner, 1985). But if structure were the only way to define social living, there would be no change, room for growth, or transformation of the human condition. "Life as series and structure of status incumbencies inhibits the full utilization of human capacities" (Turner, V., 1974, p. 242). The rituals are an opportunity to "cut loose" from this formal, rigid structure. Ritualization can be a catalyst to rearrange the structure by introducing paradox, confusion, change, and dynamism into an otherwise static structure-determined environment.

When one observes rituals and theorizes about their purposes and consequences, one can overemphasize their connection to the institutional structure. The role of rituals in perpetuating the structure can be more visible than the anti-structure or communitas of the event. But, as Turner discussed, there are other processes at work during rituals that are related to the anti-structure side of social life. What cannot be ignored in the formal theorizing about the consequences of rituals are their characteristics that participants and spectators discuss most: feelings, connection to community, freedom to achieve goals, and inspiration reaped from these events. The anti-structure or communitas side of social life is where the values, emotions, and impulses reside. Perhaps rituals, more prevalent in colleges and universities than in other modern organizations, exist to counter the rational, overly cerebral tendencies of this knowledge-based enterprise.

Anti-Structure or Communitas

Victor Turner (1969) theorized about a spontaneous, immediate, elusive, seamless, and structureless phenomenon called anti-structure or communitas. Boundless, universal, and timeless, communitas is a "generic mode of human interrelatedness" (Turner, V., 1974, p. 33); "a relationship between concrete, historical, idiosyncratic individuals . . . . [a] direct, immediate and total confrontation of human identities" (1969, pp. 131-132). Communitas is associated with "spontaneity and freedom" (1974, p. 49). "Communitas . . . is not shaped by norms, it is not institutionalized, it is not abstract . . . . It tends to ignore, reverse, cut across, or occur outside of structural relationships" (p. 274). Communitas is the undifferentiated, whole, and shared side of social living. It employs positive, generative energy to perform its work. Often present in rituals, communitas can also be triggered spontaneously during a crisis. In higher education, a death on campus or other tragic circumstance can be a catalyst for the spontaneous emotionality of communitas.

Communitas with its nondiscursive character, resides in the nonspeaking parts of our bodies and minds. With this quality, it allows elements of social living, through an evocation of feelings and thoughts not easily described, to be expressed. Evoked by the communitas of ritual, the population is homogenized in such a way that the whole of humanity is represented. Individual differences are present but, for the moment—and it is often a moment—equalized or rendered invisible.

While in this state of communitas, structural elements such as status are rejected, or deemed irrelevant, in exchange for a release of instinctual human energies. The emotional, sacred character of the communion formed between and among people during communitas takes precedence over the structure of roles and authority. One can misunderstand communitas as a time when people, messages, and emotions are coordinated in a well-planned moment. In actuality, communitas is explosive, exhilarating, and frightening. During communitas emotions take over and move rapidly through ritual participants. When the symbols, language, and action of ritual fire, a spontaneous peak is reached and a wave of emotion, oneness, and community sweeps through the audience. This moment cannot be structured but, spontaneous and unplanned, is a time when "we are one," no longer separate, unattached individuals. The strength of communitas flows during cultural events such as rituals that have "unprecedented potency" (Turner, V., 1969, p. 128).

During the Alumnae Parade and Laurel Chain at Mount Holyoke College, communitas was engendered as the senior class marched through throngs of similarly dressed alumnae. Despite the differences in age and experience, the women lining the parade route and marching through the "long white line" were temporarily one. Age, economic status, race, personal interests, and individual differences disappeared as the women, dressed in homogenizing white, were first and foremost more similar than different. Despite their extraordinary achievements as individuals, their primary identity at that unifying moment was their association with the college and to one another. At the moment of communitas, nothing else mattered.

Communitas is discussed as a normative experience where people "seek the glow of communitas among those with whom they share some cultural or biological feature to take to be their most signal mark of identity" (Turner, V., 1977a, p. 47). As such communitas compels a cultural similarity that can lead to ethnocentrism and a denial of diversity. Rather than promoting unity and communal oneness, communitas can exclude people like students of color who, during the powerful moments of communitas, may feel profound differences, not unity, with the dominant culture of the community in which they live.

Turner did not discuss how or if communitas can be manipulated, abused, and employed as a controlling device by charismatic leaders but the possibility for abuse is clearly an aspect of this emotionally charged moment. Communitas can convince one of a communal unity and similarity of purpose that then discourages disagreement, outliers, and differences from the norm.

Communitas unites human beings. Through ritual action and the ensuing communitas, people are reminded that the authoritarian levels of hierarchy are make-believe, the castelike categories into which we assign ourselves and others are a product of the imagination, and the value we place on items such as education are humanly, not naturally, designated. The moments of communitas during ritual allow participants and audience members to envision those roles as contrived and of little consequence in relationship to the grandeur of the universe and human existence. Without communitas uniting humans at a basic emotional, spiritual level, the abstract structure of social living would gain more strength and reality than it deserves.

If communitas did not interrupt structure, elements of human living would be forsaken. In higher education, the hope that everyone is similar in their ability to grow through education could be lost. Access to higher education as a worthy goal regardless of one's background could diminish. The value of education as a spiritual rather than vocational or materialistic pursuit could evaporate.

The interruption of structure by communitas points to the dynamic interplay between the two. Communitas and structure exist in tension with each other; they cannot be understood as separate entities. Through cultural processes such as ritual, structure becomes anti-structure and vice versa. "The spontaneous forms of communitas are converted into institutionalized structure, or become routinized, often as ritual" (Turner, V., 1974, p. 248). Communitas opens up possibilities to offer unconventional interpretations of social living, and structure provides a template upon which disparate interpretations occur.

Communitas in Higher Education. The boundless, universal, and timeless quality of communitas corresponds to the traditional, religious legacy of higher education. In the past, the pursuit of intellectual endeavors was reserved for cloistered monks and religious persons. Colleges and universities are charged with the pursuit of learning, a more abstract purpose than that embraced by corporations and other secular institutions. In fact, one could argue that higher education institutions are soaked in communitas and that this aspect of social living finds its most apt expression through the rituals common to those institutions.

"Communitas in ritual can only be evoked easily when there are many occasions outside the ritual on which communitas has been achieved" (Turner, V., 1974, p. 56). This viewpoint explains why so many rituals fail to fire or resist transportation from campus to campus. The success of rituals depends on the existence of communitas within the cultural context, "a bond uniting . . . people over and above any formal social bonds" (p. 45). Communitas must exist in the places and niches of the community as well as during ritual.

Mount Holyoke College, the original site for research depicted in this book, has a long history of rituals. By their admission, no one did rituals the way Mount Holyoke did. Turner's theorizing provides an explanation for their phenomenal success with these cultural marvels. Connection, devotion, emotion, and support, which pertain to communitas, were strongly encouraged. The communitas generated in settings outside the rituals allowed communitas to be created within the rituals. The communitas of the rituals spilled over into daily social living and the communitas of social living served as a foundation for the rituals.

The most significant example of communitas from the research conducted for this book was during the Alumnae Parade and Laurel Chain at Mount Holyoke College. This annual event (described as a case study in this book) is an intensely emotional and sentimental ritual. Graduating seniors march through a line of alumnae—including women who had graduated fifty years prior—carrying a laurel chain to be decked on the iron fence of the founder's grave. Standing near the parade, one can feel the palatable emotions that ripple through the crowd as the seniors approach the grave. When they lift the laurel over their heads to place it on the wrought iron fence, the feelings are particularly lush. The combination of the similarly dressed seniors and alumnae and the chain of laurel that corrals the students around the grave creates a feeling of unity and oneness that is rarely duplicated in other rituals.

The Laurel Chain and Alumnae Parade at Mount Holyoke College provides an excellent example of how anti-structure or communitas becomes structure. Ritual creates the opportunity to tell stories. These stories, such as the founding of Mount Holyoke College by Mary Lyon, become part of the sacred history of an institution.

As time progresses and the rituals are reenacted, the sacred history "becomes increasingly resistant to criticism and revision and consolidates into structure" (Turner, V., 1974, p. 249). Social systems of community living become more stable as the history gets incorporated into the structure. All members of the community, young and old, play a part in this process. "Each society requires of its mature members not only adherence to rules and patterns but at least a certain level of skepticism and initiative" (p. 256).

During ritual, this skepticism and initiative is often not explicit. Rituals do not deliver their message without ambiguity. Messages are not handed to participants in a clear, straightforward manner but, instead, are teased out. Participants are required to interpret their own meaning, perform their own thinking to attain the full experience of the ritual. The administrators and faculty who plan and carry out campus rituals realize that students are bound for an ambiguous world after graduation. This world is unsafe in the sense that there are few easy answers, and hard work is required to obtain rewards. The students learn to manage the danger of the noncampus world through the problems posed during rituals.

The work required during ritual points to the pedagogical function of communitas. People emerge from ritual with a larger, wiser perspective on life (Raybin, 1990). The ritual provides knowledge they can fold into their experiences and identity. They experience a model upon which to base their actions and life. In this way, individual and collective identity building becomes a mutually shaping process.

Communitas and Rituals of Resistance. Subversiveness or lack of self-control expressed in student rituals such as Greek hazing, the antics of Harvard's Hasty Pudding, and the abolished Kakewalk at the University of Vermont express negative anti-structure. The tenacity of these negative campus events speaks to the importance of the role they play in the social structure. It is essential that the structure side of higher education not be emphasized to the detriment of anti-structure. The positive anti-structure of social life must be expressed or it will leak out in these negative events (Manning, 1993; Manning & Eaton, 1993).

A means to express subversiveness in a way that builds positive communitas is through laughter and humor. These play an extremely important role in rituals of resistance. Laughter, especially in a setting like Mount Holyoke College's Junior Show (see case study in this book), takes the sting off the arduousness inherent in an academically rigorous setting. The laughter created and humor used in such rituals is not meant to demonstrate disrespect as much as to soften the blow.

LIMINALITY

Victor Turner (1969), expanded van Gennep's liminal or transition stage by considering liminality as a ritual quality. Conducive to generating communitas, liminality is collective, plural, fragmentary, and experimental (Turner, V., 1977b). Liminal phenomena constitute ambiguous ideas, sacred symbols, fertile nothingness, and chaos (Turner & Turner, 1985): "any condition outside, or on the peripheries of, everyday life" (Turner, V., 1974, p. 53). Liminality is different in complex societies and less complex ones (Turner & Turner). Status is more important than kinship roles; the division of labor is precise; obligations are more related to social relationships and contracts than to family or tradition; rational, bureaucratic processes rather than loyalty are at work. But, most important, particularly in complex societies where knowledge is generated at increasingly higher rates and social roles are complex, liminality is no longer contained in the times and places of cultural events such as rituals, "rather it is scattered; its remnants are everywhere" (Grimes, 1990, p. 145). The leaking of anti-structure into structure creates a severe risk for society. When the ambiguity and uncertainty of communitas characterizes everyday life rather than the contained spaces and time of rituals, chaos is not far behind.

Liminal Roles or Status

Liminal processes have the ability to reduce participants to a novice status. Liminars are no longer rivals, best friends, or neighbors. Undergoing the same ritual, liminality creates equal positions. This stripping down of liminal ritual processes simplifies and homogenizes the social structure. Obligations and complex relationships such as family are reduced to the most rudimentary of social structures.

Liminality as a Process and Space

Working from van Gennep's (1960) concept, Turner envisioned liminality as a process and space in ritual. Liminal space is "betwixt and between" (Turner, V., 1969, p. 107) social roles (child and adult, student and adult). Rituals are performances during which people are transformed from role to role. Liminality is often created during ritual by the establishment of sacred time (see chapter 9). While this characteristic of liminality resembles the transition stage of rites of passage, the similarity ends there.

In postindustrial, Western society, liminality is related to leisure, play, flow, and communitas rather than the rites of passage liminal stage that is related to the religious and universal. Sites of higher education liminal activity include initiations, fraternities, secret societies, and academic rites of passage (Turner, V., 1977b): "gatherings of alumni on American campuses in the summer, a liminoid time of leisure" (p. 47).

As a process, liminality is a release from normal constraints, a deconstruction of the constrictions of common sense, and an introduction of new ways of viewing the social structure. New constructions, freedom, and indeterminacy within the culturally constructed social world can be revealed in the moments of liminality (Turner & Turner, 1985).

Liminality, the place "betwixt and between" social roles, is possible for ritual participants because they occupy a space in the interstices or margins of the social structure. They are "outsiders" or "marginals" to the social structure and can, therefore, view that structure from the "outside" (Raybin, 1990). Liminal outsiders and marginals exist in this space so that they can speculate about "ultimate things" (Turner, V., 1974). Seeing the structure from outside or, at the very least, from the margins, can trigger the reflexive process. "Major liminal situations are occasions on which a society, *takes cognizance of itself* . . . where . . . members of that society may obtain an approximation, however limited, to a global view of man's [sic] place in the cosmos and his relations with other classes of visible and invisible entities" (p. 240). Major liminal situations in higher education include any campus-wide ritual such as centennial celebrations, commencement, or presidential inaugurations in which the entire community is engaged. These events are exceptions to the daily social structure. Performed only during exceptional occasions such as anniversaries or milestones, they create a marginal situation. Communitas is triggered in the liminal space. During these events, the community views itself as part of the whole. This whole is not just the higher education system generally but the whole "cosmos."

Transformations in Liminal Space

During ritual, when normal time and space are distorted, poised for transformation, one straddles two or more views of the self. Ritual, by making different possibilities known, creates an opportunity for the participant to suspend belief as he or she occupies liminal space, a place between the considered roles. While in liminal space, the ritual participant can make choices, retreat to old roles, or move ahead to the next stage, self, or place. Liminal time is an opportunity for contemplation, and often discussion, about choice. The discussion can include what one believes and what one will believe.

Liminality is an opportunity for transition, transformation, and provocation (Grimes, 1990). The ritual performers push the participants into liminal ground or location where they pivot between one role and another, one state and another. Liminality is most obvious during this pivot between human roles. This push is achieved through language, symbols, music, and movement, among other ritual actions. The participants evoke liminality in order to examine relationships, effect social change, reinforce social structures, and bring about individual growth. The danger inherent in the ritual process, particularly the liminal aspects, is an ineffective ritual action. Evoking liminality is dangerous business because anything can happen in the liminal area "betwixt and between" (Turner, V., 1974).

Liminality, liminal space and time are marginal through their unstructured, undefined, and often dangerous potential for success and failure (Turner, T., 1977; Turner, V., 1969). The language, symbols, and behavior of ritual often characterize or encourage the transformation from one role (e.g., student) to another (e.g., graduate). "Liminal spaces are those that bring together and mix contrary or incompatible but meaningful categories" (Morgan, 1984, p. 89). They are simultaneously in and out of the community; they occupy the cusp between roles and, as such, are paradoxically both and neither.

After the liminal state is resolved, the ritual participants are expected to follow the norms and ethical standards of their new position (Turner, V., 1969). Convocation participants are now expected to be full-fledged community members; freshly inaugurated college presidents are to act according to their new role; graduates are to enter the world of working adults.

Liminality and Emotion

Liminal aspects of rituals are deeply emotional. The evocation of emotion during the liminal processes of ritual is essential if a person is to be transformed in his or her role, place in time, or attitude. Liminality involves an emotional peak upon which a ritual participant stands as he or she is transformed, acquires new knowledge, or becomes a community member. Without evocative language, symbols, and behavior, rituals are meaningless, flat, and uninteresting. "Numinous emotions are . . . responses to a sense of some sort of extraordinary presence in which, although it is sometimes conceived to be 'wholly other,' ritual performers may feel they are participating" (Rappaport, 1992, p. 20).

TURNER'S CONCEPTS AND HIGHER EDUCATION RITUALS

Turner's concepts including liminality and identity transformation, uncertainty and transition, and cohesion can be applied to higher education. The following section suggests several of connections to his theory.

Liminality and Identity Transformation

Liminality can be viewed in light of higher education student development literature. Chickering (1969) theorized that students undergo changes in college which cause them to develop, among other attributes, autonomy, purpose, integrity, and competence. The four to six years in college comprise a liminal stage or period of a person's life when he or she is poised between the various stages of life: learner and teacher, dependent and independent. Students walk in several worlds as they live according to their independent lifestyles of the campus yet depend on their parents for tuition, guidance, and advice.

Uncertainty and Transition

Turner's concept of rituals provides a great deal of hope for the complex, conflicting relationships within higher education. Higher education's historical use of rituals and traditions provides a means to resolve current conflicts plaguing this educational system. Whether through financial crisis, reorganization and downsizing, or loss of the public trust, higher education is in a state marked by the liminal characteristics of uncertainty and transition.

Cohesion

There has not been another time in higher education where the issues of purpose, cohesion, and unity were such pressing issues. Turner's insight that conflict is the antithesis of cohesion can assist higher education administrators to identify a mechanism for healing the breach currently exposed. The informal, primordial bonds that exist in communitas can counteract the forces pushing the system toward crisis. The "undifferentiated, equalitarian, direct, nonrational" (1974, p. 47) aspects at work in communitas and anti-structure can serve higher education well if they are allowed to do their work through rituals.

SUMMARY

This chapter applied Victor Turner's work on communitas, structure, and liminality to higher education rituals. Related closely to the topics of symbols, root metaphors, and paradigms, his ideas will be further discussed in chapter 11.

Chapter 8

Baccalaureate

"This is the threshold of your lives."
—Faculty speaker, Baccalaureate

Academic regalia was as hard to manage today as it can be on any commencement day. Seniors wore the now familiar caps and gowns as they had for Fall and Second Convocations, Founder's Day, and the mischievous pranks of Disorientation. For commencement, academic hoods and collars were added to their regalia. The extra pieces of fabric were cause for confusion in the morning ritual of robing for Baccalaureate and Commencement. Few if any of the seniors actually knew what they were supposed to do, what regalia pieces they were supposed to wear for what ceremony, what body part the bits of material fit. They helped each other with safety pins or an extra pair of hands.

The moment was bittersweet because Baccalaureate was the last time the seniors would gather as a class before their graduation ceremony later that day. Baccalaureate was a moving ceremony, in part because it was held in the college chapel. The ceremony consisted of language and actions consciously focused on them, the graduating class. Seating was limited and available only by ticket for parents and guests. Given the few admissions tickets for the event, it was very likely that most seniors had not attended a Baccalaureate service prior to their own.

Baccalaureate, although retaining its religious overtones through its location in the chapel and spoken invocations by the dean of the college chapel, had been secular for years. Formalized religion was less acceptable now than in the days when Mary Lyon had established the college's evangelical mission. The chapel, featured prominently by its central location and constant use, was one of the last vestiges of Mount Holyoke's religious past.

The audience of parents, friends, and guests formed a long line snaking from the chapel door, through the college grove, to the dormitories. One had to arrive early with admission ticket in hand to be guaranteed a seat.

Some families, uninterested in the coveted inside view, staked out a spot in the folding chairs on the grass in front of the chapel's imposing double doors. The children hanging on the back of the chairs and older relatives sitting in comfortable dignity appeared to prefer the outdoor informality to the stuffy indoor vantage point.

Sitting in the air washed clean after three days of event-threatening rain was preferred to the closed-circuit television view from the campus's main auditorium. Loudspeakers would carry the words and music of the ritual to them. The ropes around their chairs gave them a sense of privacy from the spectators wandering through the trees.

College administrators and ushers dressed in white checked tickets and kept an eye on the rapidly depleting seating. With at least one hundred people left on line, the word was passed that the chapel was full. Families, courteously invited to this ritual meant for seniors, had traveled a long way for this weekend of the Alumnae Parade, Laurel Chain, Baccalaureate, and Commencement. Rumblings of dissatisfaction moved through those remaining on line as entry was halted.

Baccalaureate was the second event held in the chapel that morning. Alumnae, arriving on campus two days earlier and staying in the dormitories, had been summoned to morning services earlier that day by the pealing of the tower bell. That tolling bell signaled the commencement of most campus-wide events. But now, alumnae were nowhere in sight among the seniors and families who filled the grove. They had their own Alumnae Weekend activities to attend and acquaintances to renew.

Inside the chapel, the glee club members, looking bored, sat in their place of honor in the chancel as the guests made their way to their seats. The conductor, customarily in slacks and an oversized blouse that freed her arms for enthusiastic conducting, had also donned regalia. The bright pink chevrons on her sleeves contrasted with the silver grey of her hair.

The clear sounds of the English Handbell Choir filtered through the chapel before one realized that the women, their gloved hands holding the bells upright, stood in the balcony. Nestled under the prodigious organ pipes, they coordinated their movements to produce the rich, piercingly beautiful music. The sounds of the bells were as crisp as the choir's black and white outfits. The sound of those bells set the emotional tone for the ceremony at the same time it announced that it was beginning.

The faculty marshal who led so many faculty processions now led the seniors into the chapel for the Baccalaureate ceremony. The symbolism was clear. The seniors were approaching a turn in the road where they would be transformed from students to educated women. The marshal's honor of leading the faculty at previous events changed to the honor of leading the graduating seniors. Her pace was measured against the organ's musical backdrop. Class officers counted the seniors into rows, crowding them into the too few pews. Even with the care of these officers, empty rows were left after the last senior was in place. Ignoring the formality of the occasion, crowded seniors assertively stretched out into the vacant rows.

"Sometimes I feel like a motherless child . . . " The lyrics of the glee club's selection were a contradiction in this place where motherlike nurturing and support were so readily available. The words of the spiritual, so different in tone and meaning than that of the handbell choir, washed over the seniors and their guests.

As the ritual progressed, an alumna and member of this graduating class who had completed her classes a semester earlier moved to the center of the chancel. She was familiar to the class as one who had sung her South American songs at other campus rituals. She had set an example through her work with local Hispanic community organizations and was outspoken in her approach to social justice and peace. Although asked to sing, she took the opportunity to say a few words to her class before her performance. She spoke without the microphone close to her side, and only a word or two could be heard by the guests who sat in the pews behind the seniors, in the chapel's transepts, or in the balcony. The laughter and clapping of the students revealed that "the seniors could hear me and that's who I was talking to."

Although invited to sing solo, the woman activist had invited "a few friends" to join her. Eight African American women left their seats in the pews to join the soloist in the chancel. Ignoring their ritualistic regalia, the nine women sat comfortably on the steps leading to the chapel's altar. They jubilantly sang the words of a song by a popular feminist group, Sweet Honey and the Rock, "We who believe in freedom cannot rest until it comes." Their voices asked for commitment and social justice with an authentic soulfulness difficult for most to convey with genuineness. Without amplification, their voices filled the cavernous chapel. The bodies crowded into the pews could not muffle their words. "We who believe in freedom cannot rest until it comes."

They were a class who had come through four years together. They knew the women sitting on those steps as different from one another yet united in their attachment to the college. The students consistently and openly acknowledged the college's problems concerning racial and religious diversity. They did not know the answers to the challenges and struggles that their differences created but they cared and were working toward solutions.

The last note had barely left their mouths when the senior class leaped to their feet in ovation. The thunderous clapping and resounding cheers acknowledged the meaning of the song and appropriateness of the impromptu invitation. They were a class united through their experiences of the last four years. It was a feeling aptly described by the president: "When we come together . . . we have the one moment when the community, as one, coalesces." That moment was effervescent; one felt the emotions in the air.

The drive to continue ritual such as Baccalaureate was not fueled simply by momentum from the past. The emotions, symbols, and messages of the ritual build an emotional commitment. To feel and say the words one does during ritual is an essential part of students' college experience. Often during ritual, the good of the whole becomes more important than the individual. Students dress up, listen, sit through lengthy rites, and recite only partially believable words in return for the emotions and feeling of oneness.

The first of four speakers, three faculty members and one senior, stood to address the class. "We have tried, while you were here, to tend your mind. We . . . hope that you have learned also to tend your heart." The word "tend" was used often in this college. College participants attributed its use to the fact that women are more inclined to care for one another in a supportive way. At Mount Holyoke the dormitories and atmosphere were constructed in a deliberate manner to create an environment that tended and healed. This environment with its fertile cycle of birth, life, death, and rebirth found expression during Baccalaureate through the words of a faculty member's poem, given voice by his colleague. "Again, again, again," the poem affirmed the past while forecasting the cyclical reality of life through a return to past issues in the future.

Mount Holyoke is a community where humor reigns supreme. Not simply reserved for the informal rituals of undergraduate life, it was shared by faculty during this pre-Commencement ritual. A religion faculty speaker assured his audience, "You have been told that you are lovely, privileged, a pest, convoluted, smart, a failure . . . a woman." His words conveyed the impression that faculty as well as students were challenged in the college's environment. Furthermore, he said, "You are on the threshold of authentic self-discovery." His message to the students was about their identity. The threshold upon which they stood would be successfully transcended by discovering who they were. No one could define that for them. The seniors had to define themselves. He assured them this process of self-identification and discovery would take time.

These seniors spent four years studying academic disciplines, learning about themselves through relationships in the dormitories, and stretching their hearts and minds through the challenges of being a student at Mount Holyoke. The messages being given in the speeches of Baccalaureate were spoken one more time just in case they had been missed over the years. There was a tinge of desperation in the speakers' voices. They knew that the role of student for these women was coming to an end. The messages, "Don't confuse who you are with *what* you are," "Know who you are," "Take time," "Remember us," were stripped of their usual symbolism and obtuse ritualistic language. The speakers were clearly giving final advice before the women were launched out of the college's gates and into the real world. The college, according to the senior speaker and president of student government association, was "very much like the 'real world.' The one we believe we aren't in until this evening."

Another Baccalaureate speaker, a political science professor, had a different message for the seniors. Her message of parting was about the responsibility that accompanies their educated selves. Tuition was not the only price they would pay for the knowledge they gained at Mount Holyoke. She reminded them of the college's founding ideal of community service. She defined this community as a global one racked with the pain of AIDS, nuclear weapons, battered women, and poverty. Her words, not despairing, were spoken with a courage grounded in the conviction that these well-educated women would help rather than hinder the solutions to these problems. Her words, convincingly persuasive, engendered courage in her listeners and inspired them to move on to their life's work. She told the seniors that she hoped their "education will rest lightly on your shoulders—not a burden to yourself or others."

Baccalaureate, more than any ritual in the student's career at Mount Holyoke was, in the words of one of the speakers, a "threshold in your lives." The student walked in through the chapel doors an undergraduate student. As she walked back through those doors on her way to commencement, she was minutes away from leaving the comfortable, challenging, supportive world "inside the gates" of Mount Holyoke College. The religion professor verbalized the obviously anxious feelings of the seniors: "Today's ceremonies mark a critical rite of passage." His recommendations were to cast off naivete as they, college graduates, were expected to be wise. They were expected to be educated after four years and such high tuition. The seniors broke into wild applause at the acknowledgment of the cost of their college education.

The turn in the road, in sight as the seniors marched up the aisle to their pews, came more clearly into view as the ritual progressed. The political science professor ushered the seniors into the ranks of the educated with her words, "we all are . . ." as opposed to the usual, "you all are . . ." The distance between educated person, as represented by the faculty member, and student was reduced to nonexistent.

The final speaker, a senior chosen by her class to speak with the faculty members, was the president of the student government association. She had distinguished herself throughout her years as a student and stood proudly in the pulpit. Her speech had a more personal ring as she addressed the seniors. She was not one toward whom they walked but one with whom they stood. Using the gate metaphor so often evoked at Mount Holyoke to depict the college's unique environment, she spoke about their prospects "as we walk out of Mount Holyoke's gates today." She reflected back on their four years: the divestment of stocks with South African connections, the questioning of the single-sex mission as a sister college turned coeducational, and the all-campus meeting about racism. She showed her personal growth concerning racial diversity as she assured her classmates that "we cannot nor can we claim to know everything about other people." But, building on the feeling created by the African American women who so jubilantly sang the enthusiastically received song of hope, the student speaker assured her audience that they were moving in the right direction.

The seniors listened intently as the four invited speakers addressed the audience. As always, their heads occasionally came together in whispered closeness. A feeling of expectation and thick emotionalism hung in the air. The audience sitting behind the seniors might well have been absent. The speakers and seniors were absorbed in their own dialogue based on the messages of the college community.

The seniors stood in ovation as the speakers finished. Each speaker gave a different voice to the ideals and traditions of the college. Adapting the rules of etiquette, the guests remained in their seats. The recognition and thanks represented by the standing women was to be conveyed by them alone. Seniors thanked the speakers they had expressly chosen to speak during Baccalaureate. But, through the ovation these students were clearly giving thanks to the entire college for the four years of effort expended on them.

As the seniors paraded out of the chapel with only one more college ritual to experience, the audience stood in respectful silence. A senior respondent, in describing the feelings that the students had for the college, said, "I don't hear people talking about their schools like this." She was referring to the pride and commitment expressed by even the most cynical students. Baccalaureate added to the stock of stories and memories that the students collected over their four years.

These rituals were important in the business of creating a campus sisterhood, pulling the community together, and creating the feeling that "we are one."

THEMES WITHIN BACCALAUREATE

The language and actions of Baccalaureate were moving and evocative. The emotional expression, already at a peak as the event began, built through the ritual as it had in the days and weeks prior to commencement. Four years of shared experiences, close friendships, and academic progress climaxed in Baccalaureate. The limited seating and intentionally designed elements of the event (e.g., recitation of a faculty member's poem, candid statements about campus struggles with racism) added to the emotional nature of Baccalaureate.

A Private Ceremony

Several respondents commented on the private nature of Baccalaureate. The speakers did not disregard the guests and families in attendance but directed their messages to the seniors. These invited speakers summarized the college experience and reinforced the messages learned over the students' four years of college. The speeches told stories of their times and experiences as a class. The expression of mutual experiences, common language expressed through "we" and "our," and shared thoughts about their accomplishments and futures expressed the collective dimension of the ritual. The messages portrayed in the speeches (what "we" have learned), the songs (courage and compassion), and the symbols aimed to assure the identity of the seniors as individuals and as a class.

Baccalaureate Communitas

Communitas occurred during the ovation that erupted after the African American women's song. The words of their song, "We who believe in freedom cannot rest until it comes," the impromptu invitation to the all-Black gospel choir by the scheduled singer, the casual way they sat on the chancel steps, and the powerful lyrics sung directly to the seniors led to a tremendous outpouring of emotion. The moment summarized the joy and challenge this class faced as students.

Passage Between States

Flanigan discussed the importance of the presence of two elements in rituals that were very much a part of Baccalaureate: processions and choirs. "Processions . . . [are] a common and important form of ritual action" (1990, p. 50). They represent "passage from one stage of life to another" (p. 50). As such, they symbolically represent the passage that van Gennep (1960) outlined in detail in his classic *Rites of Passage*. During many rituals such as commencements, baccalaureates, inaugurations, and even building dedications, processions, particularly with faculty and administration attired in regalia, signal the audience that the ritual, the performance through which the change from one state of life to another will take place, has begun. Many rituals such as Baccalaureate reverse the order of the processional participants to signal that, following the ritual, a change has occurred. Faculty and administration who process in first at the beginning of the ritual, followed by students, are often asked to wait until the students (now graduates) have the honor of processing out before the faculty.

Processions as in the Baccalaureate ritual described above are no exception. They "served the ritual purpose of establishing and reinforcing the prevailing political order" (Flanigan, 1990, p. 51). Therefore, the order of the procession of faculty, administrators, platform party, and students was no accident. The order reinforced, or in a ritualistic sense reversed, the political order present in the institutional structure.

Transition and Transformation

More than any other ritual observed during the research, Baccalaureate contained the elements of change and transition characterized in van Gennep's (1960) rites of passage. The speakers' language placed particular emphasis on transformation from senior to graduate, student to educated woman, and inside-the-college to outside-world dweller. Specifically, phrases such as "inside these gates . . . outside these gates" and "as we walk out of Mount Holyoke's gates today" created the impression that change was imminent and constant throughout the course of the ritual.

Tending and Care

The language of Baccalaureate emphasized the tending that was so much a part of these students' education and growth processes at the college. Growth was expected to occur in emotional and personal as well as academic and professional ways. The metaphors liberally sprinkled through the speeches ("bulging knapsacks," students disguised as children, and "motherless child") alluded to the growth that occurred during the students' college years.

SUMMARY

Baccalaureate served as a capstone experience and occasion to summarize the students' college years. The practice of teaching leadership through discovery and support was replaced with a final effort to explicitly describe the goals, messages, and purpose of the education the seniors completed. The style clearly indicated the messages intended by the faculty and administration: achievement, growth, self-esteem, and diversity.

Chapter 9

Cultural Performances: Rehearsals and Informality

> There are no clear boundaries to conclusively limit and define cultural performance. Ritual certainly has its complexities, but they are of a different order from these more scattered, fragmentary, and partial orderings which give coherence to social life (Rabinow, 1977, p. 58).

Student shows, receptions, theater shows, carnivals, parades, and community celebrations such as fairs and picnics are part and parcel of campus life. These events have a ritual-like character despite the fact that they do not fit the prescribed definition of rites of passage or secular ceremony. Rather, their informal structure, loosely scripted action, and evocative emotional quality meet the definition of cultural performances as advanced by John MacAloon (1984). These campus traditions lack a formal script and plot, routinized behaviors, exaggerated action, or the pivot point of rites of passage (Moore & Myerhoff, 1977; van Gennep, 1960). But they communicate crucial meaning and are linked to strong emotions essential to cultural communities.

CULTURAL PERFORMANCES CHARACTERISTICS

Cultural performances, resembling rehearsal rather than the polished performance of a rite of passage or ceremony, create opportunities to express ideas and communicate meaning. These often ludicrous, playful events "are more than entertainment, more than didactic or persuasive formulations, and more than cathartic indulgences. They are occasions in which as a culture or society we reflect upon and define ourselves with alternatives, and eventually change in some ways while remaining the same in others" (MacAloon, 1984, p. 1). Cultural performances, a celebration of community, spark a liminal spontaneity that acclaims people, places, symbols, and relationships. Through these activities, definitions about the "way things are supposed to be" are challenged. Messages presented in a fun-loving, self-critical manner emphasize alternatives to accepted practice.

As events that communicate meaning, picnics, community gatherings, and impromptu celebrations make statements, verbal and nonverbal, about community life. In colleges and universities, these events eloquently yet informally express the community's identity, founding beliefs, and fundamental values. This communication adds unity and cohesion to campus life that would otherwise be diffused and scattered.

MacAloon's (1984) discussion of cultural performances provides insight about the traditions occurring in higher education. Though less formally developed than theory about rites of passage or secular ceremony, the cultural performances definition and concept can assist higher education administrators, students, and faculty in considering human actions that are performative yet spontaneous and informal. His explanation is particularly important because events that fit his definition are predominantly student initiated. MacAloon's interpretation of cultural performances is useful in understanding events more meaningful to students than others. The characteristics of cultural performances determined through this ritual research expands MacAloon's discussion to include informal structure, inconsistent repetition, non-routinized action, evocative style, and simple staging.

Informal Structure

Cultural performances do not rely on formal structure or form to communicate their intent. Campus ideals, mission, purpose, and community meaning are communicated during cultural performances through immediacy, simplicity, and gaiety. With less emphasis on form and function and more on making a convincing evocation, cultural performances tap the full range of ritual action.

In keeping with their informal structure, cultural performances circumvent formal dress, methodical processionals, and prescribed behavior. The informal structure adds to the emotionally charged experiences of cultural performances.

Inconsistent Repetition

Cultural performances use repetition of action and symbols in a less orderly manner than rites of passage or secular ceremonies. Actions and symbols may be used from previous performances, or event participants may haphazardly modify their use in an adapted performance. The form of the performance can remain the same from year to year, change significantly in subsequent performances, or recycle back to an earlier form. There may or may not be any rhyme or reason for these changes, which can result from faulty memory, individual preferences, or even disrespect for past tradition. Ritual and ceremonial precision of dress, actions, and language gives way in cultural performances to informal, powerful actions that open participants to an array of cultural meaning.

A cultural performance is "an interrogation of, dialogue with a cultural constrained set of materials and tools" (Babcock, 1984, p. 106). The materials and tools of cultural performances take on cultural meaning from prior events as well as from their connection to the meaning possessed by higher education. During Junior Show at Mount Holyoke College, a costume of a griffin (a mythical beast with head and wings of an eagle and the body of a lion) was worn by a performer. The griffin was the symbol of the class sponsoring the show, so therefore it had significant cultural meaning. In addition to the immediate cultural meaning, the costume had been worn by a member of the Class of 1914 at her Junior Show. The costume was eighty years old. Its age and association with generations of alumnae endowed the costume with even more cultural value.

Adapting the form, costumes, words, and actions of preceding community members involves "appropriating, absorbing, transforming the texts of others" (Babcock, 1984, p. 107). Text in this context means the cultural belief, values, and ideals of the college community. Appropriation of texts during a cultural performance such as Junior Show can entail using a public community member's (e.g., a college president's) words or mannerisms in parody. This use during a presentation like Junior Show draws the leader into students' lives.

One can never be sure what will transpire during a cultural performance. Stories of prior enactments offer clues for understanding and interpretation. Observations and conclusions about the current performance fold into previous stories. The lessons learned through the interpretation and meaning making of cultural performances become a theoretical template upon which to interpret subsequent events. Student action borrowed from community texts is transformed into cultural capital.

Stories of the humorous appropriation are passed from generation to generations; folded into the cultural capital of the community. Such text appropriation, in a positive sense, unites the community as presidential action is employed and transformed by the students. The separation between student and administrator is reduced as students adopt the president's words as their own.

Nonroutinized Action

The formal script, score, and stylized action of rites of passage and secular ceremony are absent during cultural performances. The nonroutine action creates an atmosphere of uncertainty and apprehension. Without the prescribed behavior of prior enactments, any action or behavior is possible. Furthermore, the playfulness and celebrative nature of cultural performances create an attitude of anticipation. When the cultural performance is prefaced with stories of hilarious past enactments, expectations may run very high.

Participants approach cultural performances with tentativeness and uneasiness. Students, particularly those new to the college, often approach cultural performances with a naive tentativeness. Not sure what these events entail, lacking information about the messages to be conveyed and meanings to be concluded, participants gather information, make observations, and conduct activities that are folded into their meaning-making activities. Common questions include Where do I sit? What's going to happen here? What am I supposed to get out of this? Impressions and interpretations build into theories that are then employed to interpret subsequent events and cultural performances.

Evocative Style

The evocation of emotions elicited in rites of passage and ceremonies through a presentational style is also present in cultural performances. Emotions run particularly high when the communion and celebration of common beliefs are displayed. "The investment of resources in preparation, anticipation, transportation, and admission, the social interests composing the performance's purpose, and the dramatic character of its form all contribute to the excitement already embodied potentially in its contents" (MacAloon, 1984, p. 9). Cultural performances with their informal style and evocative presentation create opportunities for a distinct expression of cultural meaning. Campus events that may be seen as a burden or unnecessary can be reinterpreted into pertinent expressions of community living.

At Mount Holyoke College, student respondents discussed the biannual community-wide picnics during which faculty, students, and staff assemble on the green and share a meal. These occasions were an infrequent opportunity for the entire community to gather. This college assembly was so essential to community solidarity that nonstudents, who did not possess a meal contract, were provided the meal free of charge as an incentive to attend. It was essential that, at some point, the community as a whole gather to share food, conversation, and each other's company.

Simple Staging

Cultural performances often take place on a "stage," consisting of no more than a space set aside from the audience (Singer, 1984). This separation, as in ritual and ceremonies, creates a sacred place in the sense that the uneventful actions of everyday life are transformed into an occasion, culturally marked as special or extraordinary. Marked by a raised platform or cordoned-off space, the presence of a simple stage informs participants that words will be shared, messages communicated. Prior experience with cultural performances instructs participants to anticipate a prescribed act more contrived than everyday action but less so than a rite of passage or secular ceremony.

HUMAN PURPOSES EXPRESSED THROUGH CULTURAL PERFORMANCES

The characteristics of cultural performances outlined above create opportunities for several human purposes to be served: fusing dichotomies, creating ritual and sacred time, power and sanctity, and generating process. These processes can be provoked through rites of passage, secular ceremonies, and cultural performances. The generic term, ritual, will be used in the following discussion to ease discussion and understanding.

Fusing Dichotomies

Dichotomies including old and new, student and administrator, and past and present are bridged through ritual action (MacAloon, 1984). In fact, ritual action can be a process of "overcoming, transcending, the powerful dichotomies" (Marcus, 1988, p. 71). Ritual action that bridges dichotomies can create circumstances of larger, more meaningful understandings (Rappaport, 1992). Higher education dichotomies present and ripe for transcendence are near and far, oral and written, public and private, doing and thinking, male and female. As these dichotomies are made visible and vocalized during cultural events they are exposed to scrutiny and discussion. Some of the dichotomies expressed and resolved through campus rituals observed in the research for this book were individual and group, past and present, higher and lower, self and other, and young and old.

Individual and Group. Rituals focus on individual and group identities through declarations of what a community believes itself to be. The group identity, forged through time and the history of a community's existence, becomes a template upon which individuals assess their actions. Individuals can assess their actions and commitments against the role models honored during award ceremonies. Stories told during an alumni panel can inspire and motivate. As individuals share their stories during the ritual, their individual histories become part of the community's history, and vice versa. Histories are shared and fused through this back and forth borrowing.

Oftentimes, the history, individual or group, can be represented in a symbol or object. The walls of college campuses are adorned with commemorative plaques, citations, and other symbols of individual and institutional history. Presidential offices and executive reception areas often contain objects representing individual achievements. The fact that these are displayed publicly allows them to be appropriated into institutional history.

The identity-defining statements of ritual are verbal as well as physical. Symbolic objects accrue cultural value over the years to represent the history, identity, and beliefs of the community. These identity-defining terms and symbols can be, among others, team mascots, nicknames, architectural figures, and school colors. One need only go to a major university's football game to see signs of institutional-identifying colors worn by avid individual fans.

This fusion of individual and group is essential to the meaning-making processes and history of the institution. Both sides of the dichotomy are utilized during rituals to build continuity. Institutional identity requires ritual practice to build coherence and legitimacy. Without rituals, this identity can be obscure, confused, and clouded. Conversely, without purpose and identity-defining rituals, individuals can have a difficult time defining their place within the institution. Through rituals and the symbols contained in them, students adopt names that indicate institutional identity (e.g., a "tarheel") and pride; the institution similarly folds individuals' experiences (accomplishments, stories) into the cache of institutional lore.

Past and Present. Repetition in rituals can fuse past and present as the same ritual is performed year after year. Despite the fact that the rituals are decidedly distinct from year to year, when a core meaning is consistently communicated, the event carries the same name or some practices are conserved, these practices create the impression that the ritual and action experienced are identical.

The Junior Show griffin costume account described above demonstrates how class color and symbol bridge dichotomies of past and present and near and far. Through ritual action, the experiences of students who attended Mount Holyoke College at distinctly different time periods were fused in time and place. This fusion was accomplished by the use of a costume from the past in a present setting. Generations of students can be fused through jointly shared events, similar experiences, and common symbols.

Higher and Lower. Theorists have written about an aspect of ritual action called inversion or reversal (Babcock, 1990). Planned or unplanned, reversals of power, status, and hierarchy are often dramatized during rituals. Students are raised to a status equal to or above the highest status members of the community during convocations. This can be achieved through assigned seats of honor, recitations of achievements, access to hallowed locations, and attention paid through ceremonial action. Privileges not usually bestowed on students and staff (canceled classes, time away from the office) are commonplace during rituals. Persons of lower status, at least temporarily, receive the rights and privileges of persons of higher status.

Reversals also occur informally through playfulness. Joking and clowning can occur during the most sacred moments of rituals (Babcock, 1984). When students clown during commencements and honors ceremonies, they usurp the business of the ritual. They take over the ritual by creating moments of hilarity passed along through institutional storytelling. This reversal of seriousness can turn the purposes of the ritual and meaning conveyed completely on end.

Self and Other. Rituals serve as a mirror upon which institutional expectations, mythical accounts, hopes, and wishes are reflected. Participants can absorb the messages and meanings of the ritual in a self-reflective process of examination and soul searching. Particularly during rituals where the feats of institutional heroes and heroines are depicted, the contrast between self and other can be revealing. Students experiencing the celebrated stories of others can imagine themselves performing similar acts. The contemplative nature of rituals creates moments during which the self can decide whether or not to follow in the footsteps of the other.

Self and other can also be fused through the pride generated in the accomplishments of the other. One need not possess the abilities or achieve the successes of the other to feel pride in their mutual community membership.

Young and Old. Ritual action—similarity of dress, action, and words intoned—can fuse young and old. Differences in age and experience recede into the background as ritual action implies that there are only similarities, no differences. When ritual action and language emphasize particular circumstances (e.g., college attendance) and role (e.g., student), age becomes irrelevant. Both young and old view their experiences as similar—even the same—when, of course, they are not. It is only during the time of the ritual that such an illusion can be created.

During the Laurel Chain and Alumnae Parade at Mount Holyoke College, seniors saw themselves, both visually and symbolically, connected to the long line of women in white who walked before them. Young and old were fused through the Parade that linked past and present students. Young and old were the "same" in dress, role, and purpose as they marched in unison toward the founder's grave.

Creating Ritual and Sacred Time

Human beings adhere to a rigid concept of time that, though it appears real, is socially constructed. Mundane time, lived every day, is punctuated with extraordinary, sacred, or "out of time" time created during rituals, ceremonies, and cultural performances. These events define and disrupt socially constructed mundane time. They put boundaries on the naturally discontinuous state of human affairs by imposing order, repeating performances, and limiting ritual behaviors to the prescribed and accepted. Rituals "sever seamless durations into distinct periods and may also invest those periods with significance" (Rappaport, 1992, p. 11).

These same events disrupt regular time by marking occasions, defining meaning, and staging exceptional performances. The daily routine is punctuated by the extraordinary. By simultaneously defining and disrupting time, these powerful occasions create a timeless quality about human action and meaning (Myerhoff, 1984).

> When successful, ritual replaces chronological, collective time with the experience of flowing duration, paced according to personal significance; sometimes this is so powerful that we are altogether freed from a sense of time and of awareness of self. This is ritual time, and it must be present to some degree to mount the mood of conviction concerning the messages contained in a ritual (p. 174).

By simultaneously defining and disrupting chronological time, rituals, ceremonies, and cultural performances create a mood of timelessness. This extraordinary time constructs the "relationships of the never-changing to the ever-changing" (Rappaport, 1992, p. 15).

Respondents in the Mount Holyoke study commented on the seamless sense of time created through the rituals and ceremonies. Because, as they commented, the rituals were always there, the timelessness discussed above was evoked. "In ritual, one returns ever again to that which never changes, to that which is punctiliously repeated in every performance" (Rappaport, 1992, p. 25). The students were linked in an extraordinary way to the time that preceded them. Current time was, during ritual, the same as the past and future.

Of course, the rituals, which the students in particular claimed as "being the same," were never exactly reproduced. They changed through deliberate action, errors in production, and faux pas, among other factors. But, because they were "always there," year after year, the rituals, ceremonies, and cultural performances created a sense of never changing continuity in an ever changing world. This flow or sense of the eternal interjects the divine into what would otherwise be temporal, routine daily living (Rappaport, 1992).

Power and Sanctity

The informal staging of cultural performances and the formal staging of secular ceremonies and rituals focus power. The "power spots" (McLaren, 1986, p. 197) created by this focus give rituals, ceremonies, and cultural performances a magical quality. Lecterns high above the audience, altars etched with symbols, centrally located stages, stained glass windows are all devices that focus power—and meaning. These power spots are easily recognizable because their sanctity or sacredness is unquestionable, unfalsifiable, and unverifiable (Rappaport, 1992).

The sanctity created is part of humankind's critical need to endow people's lives with meaning. The unbelievable *must* become believable so that ritual and community participants can accept the larger truths of life. Audiences are aware of the sanctity and power of these spaces. They indicate their reverence by refraining from walking across a stage, even before the ritual or ceremony begins. Such behavior is taboo.

Generating Process

Similar to rites of passage and ceremonies, the liminal experiences dramatized during cultural performances create situations of transformation and change. A useful way to think about rituals, ceremonies, and cultural performances is "becoming." "The social world is a world in becoming, not a world in being" (Turner, V., 1974, p. 24). The latter approach is one of process, indeterminacy, and reflexivity (Turner & Turner, 1985).

If one could stop the processual nature of rituals, ceremonies, and cultural performances to take a snapshot, "one would probably find that the temporal structures were incomplete, open-ended, unconsummated. They would be, at most, on their way to an ending" (Turner, V., 1974, p. 36). They would be in flux, incomplete, and in process. Unlike the static assumption of rites of passage or even the transformative but still stable character of secular ceremonies, cultural performances have an almost transparent image of the made-up-ness of social life as a whole. The static appearance of these events often masks their processual and dynamic nature.

> Religious and legal institutions, among others, only cease to be bundles of dead or cold rules when they are seen as phases in social processes, as dynamic patterns right from the start . . . . The formal, supposedly static, structures only become visible through this flow which energizes them, heats them to the point of visibility (p. 37).

Higher education institutions can be dead and cold without cultural aspects to enliven them. The heart of colleges and universities does not lie in the knowledge, policies, rules, and academic disciplines that make up their bureaucratic structure. What is most alive about higher education institutions is the human agency and subjectivity that underscore the action occurring within their walls.

SUMMARY

The concepts concerning cultural performances advanced by John MacAloon (1984) present interesting possibilities for understanding the informal celebrations so common on college campuses. By comprehending their purposes and actions, one can express and understand the magic and sanctity of human action.

Chapter 10

Junior Show

What you doin'?

Your schedule's tough, the thing just isn't movin,'

No time for rest.

Can't take a fever, you have got to take that test! . . .

Feel the stress it cuts like a knife.

You'll have lots of time to sleep in real life,

Look what this school has done to me,

I can't be caffeine free!!

—Lyrics from Junior Show song

The assistant to the president, an alumna administrator, described Junior Show as *"a big deal."* Past Junior Shows were the image of family entertainment with original music and lyrics and a five-piece band to provide live accompaniment for the singing and dancing. Rehearsals were planned with abundant time to execute a high-quality show.

The planning for this year's Junior Show started in January, approximately six weeks before the show. The original songs were replaced with lip-synched take-offs on the pop music heard on students' stereos and radios in the dormitories. Taped recordings of the background selections and the strength of a few women's voices held the songs and effort together.

ACADEMIC SURVIVAL THROUGH FRIENDSHIP

Junior Show belied the Mount Holyoke caricature of students who constantly studied and strove for scholarly achievement. In contrast, the performance was a break, a point where one stopped out, according to a senior respondent, "to survive something that's so challenging." These occasions were extremely meaningful. "That's one of the things that the traditions are good for," explained a senior, "They break up" the academic challenge. They are an opportunity to get together, build relationships outside the dormitories and share experiences outside the classroom.

Junior Show is more than a production. The spring ritual is *the* event that brings the junior class together as they act out the memories and milestones of their college years. Junior Show is something to rally around, a time for the class to join together. One of the writers for this particular show maintained a journal since her freshman year. This chronicle provided the content for the show as she had written down her memories of events otherwise forgotten.

Climbing up the steps to the student center one could see the lobby already packed with people waiting for the auditorium doors to open. The impatient crowd pushed aggressively. Junior Show, especially this last night, was preceded with an exciting buildup. A woman wearing the class color green leaped onto a chair and shouted to the crowd, "Stop pushing. We can still cancel the show—right now. You will all get in. We're not like this, so stop it." The crowd relaxed, surprisingly listened to her, stopped pushing, and became quiet.

Saturday, the last night of the annual production, was senior dedication night. The seats on the auditorium floor, the best in the house, were reserved for the graduating class. Attired in their class blue shirts from their Junior Show performed the previous spring, seniors had their tables staked out as they ran around visiting classmates and friends.

Shouting generated by class pride erupted between the left and right balconies as two choruses of juniors tried to outshout the cries of the seniors. The seniors had the advantage of tables to pound on but the juniors, bolstered with beer hidden behind the stage, were determined to prevail. Faculty, parents, and spectators quietly observed as class competition and rivalry reached its fevered pitch.

The rowdy behavior during Junior Show disproved the stereotypes attributed to Mount Holyoke and its students by those outside the college. A satirical piece in the student newspaper listed a few of them: "Snooties . . . easy to talk to and plan parties with, 'genuine interest in bettering the mind,' mountainy, rugged, rich snobs, monastery shut up in the woods, unshaven and unshowered women, 'convent full of lesbians someplace in the great north woods,' 'snobs' in the East." This night those stereotypes were forgotten as class competition reigned and good, clean college fun prevailed.

The academic rigor permeating the institution made Mount Holyoke a challenging place to be a student. One way to survive was to confide in friends about that struggle. These lifelong friendships were formed not just in the close living conditions of the dormitories but through events such as Junior Show. These intense friendships helped students prevail through even the worst of times and circumstances. The discomfort of such a challenging environment would be impossible without friends.

CHALLENGE AND WOMEN'S HIGHER EDUCATION

Challenge is part and parcel of women's higher education. A senior respondent described the rationale behind the challenge. The "bad times and the good times at Mount Holyoke make it easier to weather the world out there." At this college, students were pushed and tested by high expectations. "For the first time," explained an alumna administrator from the Class of '84, "I was surrounded by women of equal or greater intelligence than my own." They "gained a sense of identity and self-awareness," "were challenged intellectually and spiritually." These women were to become everything they could. That irrepressible challenge was not easy to live with on a day-to-day basis. "For some individuals it continues to haunt them" even after they graduate, further explained the non-alumna secretary of Mount Holyoke.

The intense intellectual environment provoked an interpretation about the existence of the rituals and traditions that would, admittedly, not be tolerated in other college settings. "If academics weren't so important—people wouldn't accept it," reasoned the junior class president. The rituals and traditions, high expectations, and single-sex environment took some adjustment.

RITUALS AS A PUNCTUATION

The traditions were a punctuation in the intense student lifestyle. They were an opportunity, explained the dean of college chapel, to "slow down and take time for one another." When people spend four years together, bonding occurs. It grows from nurturing one's potential and the potential of others. The students supported each other's dreams.

Class colors clashed and yelling continued as the first skit of Junior Show began. Six women sat on stage, bolstered with Diet Coke and bags of chips, struggling with ideas for a theme for their annual Junior Show. Frustrated, one of them suggested canceling the whole show. "We can't cancel Junior Show— it's a tradition!!" exclaimed the women in the skit.

Junior Show, explained a former senior class president and alumna administrator, was the one event that "really meant something to our class." Their Junior Show "was great . . . the best. It is terrific for the class. They know one another beforehand but they *really* get to know one another as they work on it."

Junior Show was one more opportunity to counterbalance the isolation of the rural environment, lack of a diverse social life, and intensity of the academic rigor. The points of balance were the passion students had for one another. The dean of students described the college community as "very alive," full of an "extraordinary joy and happiness." At Mount Holyoke, students, administrators, and faculty could openly express deep feelings for each other as well as the community. "The traditions . . . link you to those people," a senior respondent claimed. On this campus, there was no need to be shy about expressing emotion. Junior Show, similar to other rituals and traditions at Mount Holyoke, played a role in building that passion.

LAUGHING AT YOURSELF

The antics of the show continued with expressions of the caricatures that the writers developed about Mount Holyoke women. Students with little to no inhibitions dressed outrageously and danced to the predominantly female audience. Would-be actresses pranced through laundry room sets with pearls, pumps, and an affected demeanor. Rugby players disrupted aerobic classes where women earnestly tried to outpace the pounds gained through an overabundance of dining hall food and nightly "milk and crackers." The caricatures were exaggerations of parts of all of them but a full representation of very few, if any. The image beyond the caricatures was that the students worked, played, and relaxed. Yet well-worn inside jokes about Lanz nightgowns, tea and cookies, and being "genteel" were liberally sprinkled throughout the hilarious skits.

The women singing, acting, and dancing on stage were recognized by their fellow classmates who yelled their names from the floor. The jokes and malicious comments shouted from the audience indicated closeness and familiarity among the students from different classes. Unrestricted freedom was the norm as audience and participants alike yelled, let out the trademark college "whoop," and made as much noise as possible.

Arms were thrown over shoulders, hugs abounded. Women at the tables and on stage clung to each other in a visible display of affection: touching, laughing, and hugging. These women could express their feelings of joy, pride, and closeness to each other without embarrassment. They celebrated the fact that they were women, intelligent women, who could show each other affection and support. In contrast to what they expected when they graduated and entered the world of work, at this college one's womanhood was never devalued. At other schools one had to fight for the respect that was automatically expected at Mount Holyoke. A senior respondent and Black student leader reminisced that during her Fall Convocation ritual as a freshman student, she heard, "'Woman, woman,' and you look around and you think, 'Who is she talking to?' Then you realize that it's you. It's the first time that you are called a capable and viable woman."

The relationships that women formed with one another were deeply emotional. "Dare I use the word 'passionate'—in a spiritual sense" were the words used by an alumna administrator. Different from coeducational or even other single sex institutions, the passion she referred to was different in nature and "perhaps not the same as other women's institutions." This was a passion and spirituality born of women's strength through intellectual mastery and ability.

The strong relationships built at Mount Holyoke were particularly meaningful for the juniors and seniors during Junior Show as this time of year marked a turning point for both classes. Seniors realized that their time on campus was coming to an end. Juniors realized that they only had one more year to be college students.

FINALE

The sea of green on the stage matched the sea of blue on the floor as the juniors amassed on stage for the final song.

Now we've had the time of our lives,

And we hope that you've enjoyed it too.

We kept quiet, for so long,

Now we've shared it all with you . . .

So stand here side by side, and you know we've really tried to have fun . . .

So we challenge you Sophomores.

Can you rise above? . . .

Junior Show's the time of your life.

We've loved this year at Mount Holyoke.

And we've proved to ourselves,

Just how close our class can be.

At the conclusion of Junior Show, seniors and juniors met in each other's arms in an outpouring of affection and sadness. They held onto one another in what was to be one of the first of many good-byes. They knew that there was so much to say good-bye to: the other seniors, the place where they had grown so much, and the intensity of an environment that they knew did not exist outside Mount Holyoke's walls. Juniors jumped off the stage to hug seniors in the audience. Seniors jumped on the stage to hug juniors and each other. Some audience members, including seniors, observed the scene with detachment and mild interest.

The visible outpouring of emotion epitomized the campus ideal that relationships were important. A freshman respondent had already learned that her "time here depends on the people that you are with." All of this "makes special people": the friendships that are formed between people, the relationships and the bonding at Mount Holyoke.

Rituals organized solely by the students were described by a senior respondent as the "fun things." They are the events that create unity, engender passion, and build community. At this residential college they were mostly created and performed in the dormitories. They created a feeling of "home" by welcoming and orienting new students to Mount Holyoke. They were the events that helped students make sense of college life.

JUNIOR SHOW INTERPRETATIONS

A Pause or Marker in Time

Junior Show and accompanying rituals and cultural performances create opportunities for students to pause and look around them. As a marker in time, Junior Show provides an opportunity to take time from the everyday intensity and academic grind and single out the juniors and seniors for special recognition. The pause helps students recognize that there is something of consequence occurring at this college. Women gather to pause in their work to relate, talk, and just be together. The lifelong bonds and relationships formed during college were described by a senior respondent, who was cynical about the traditions but drawn into their action and messages all the same. "I know this is going to sound funny, but if I ever had a daughter I would want her to come here. It's the same with my family. My mother really wanted me to come here. She always wanted me to be a sister."

Anthropological Interpretations

Cox (in Babcock, 1984) discusses a type of cultural performance in which conscious excess, celebrative affirmation, and juxtaposition are the primary means of communication. This cultural performance, Junior Show, uses all three means to communicate messages about the campus community, engender and solidify relationships, and, most obviously, concoct fun.

Conscious Excess. Everything about Junior Show relates to conscious excess: the rabid class pride, the repetition of class colors, shouting, drinking, and emotional outbursts. Notable about this excess is the fact that it is deliberately planned into Junior Show. Because they have attended Shows in the past, students know what is expected of them when they are juniors and seniors. There are even good-natured challenges among classes to exceed the excesses of the previous class.

This expression of excess is an opportunity for human beings to cut loose. Similar to Carnival or Mardi Gras, Junior Show gives these young women, who are extremely serious about their scholarship and careers, an opportunity to misbehave. This explanation of Junior Show as conscious excess is not meant to justify similar college excesses as "good clean college fun." Many of the latter excesses, most notably the high consumption of alcohol, have led to tragic circumstances. But, part of being human means that, every once in awhile, one wants to be a bit mischievous. Whether on Halloween or during Junior Show, people want to dress up, act out the most outrageous stereotypes, or just play with personal images in ways that point to possibilities yet to be imagined.

Creative Affirmations. Junior Show was a cultural performance during which to create and enact statements about the meaning of community life. In an atmosphere of intense challenge, Junior Show could serve as an opportunity for affirmation. The major affirmation expressed during Junior Show was the feeling that the students' choice for college was correct. The passionate and intense bonding expressed during Junior Show assured them that they were in the right environment for the challenge and support they craved.

Junior Show epitomized celebrative affirmation through the vigor and candor of a women's community. Throughout Junior Show, similar to everyday campus life, emotions were celebrated through a free and open expression. In this community, women's relationships and ability to care were celebrated as an aspect of campus life as important than academic achievement.

Juxtapositions. Junior Show juxtaposed several sometimes complementary, other times paradoxical meanings: challenge *and* support were crucial, fun *and* work were a balance for which to strive, respect *and* irreverence could be playfully presented. As with other rituals and cultural performances, old and new, past and present, and young and old were also expressed. These juxtapositions were most aptly expressed through symbols. Among others, symbolic caricatures of administrators, song lyric appropriation for comical effect, and, most meaningfully for students, use of an eighty-year-old griffin costume borrowed from the Class of 1914. Symbols, because they fool our "normal" perspective, fire emotions, cause out of the ordinary reactions, or evoke a burst of emotion, are fitting carriers of meaning.

Nonpaternalism

A potent theme expressed through Junior Show was the cooperation and support present at Mount Holyoke. Numerous respondents remarked that cooperation was an essential aspect of the community. As acted out during Junior Show, one could not make it through college without the support of friends, administrators, and faculty.

This cooperation and support was seen by Mount Holyoke students as contrasting sharply with the paternalistic values of competition and detached emotions of coeducational institutions. These latter institutions, organized on paternalistic ideals of power, authority, and hierarchy (Schaef, 1985), were viewed as profoundly different in tone and character than women's institutions.

Though not completely free of paternalistic values (e.g., students resided in the lower levels of the hierarchical structure while administrators occupied the more powerful upper positions), there were significant differences at Mount Holyoke concerning power, authority, and responsibility.

An Empowered Challenge

Students independently assumed and/or were expected by administrators to accept responsibility for Mount Holyoke's ideals. Students challenged each other, the faculty, alumnae, and administration to assume leadership and world citizenship. This challenge was non-paternalistically issued through empowerment, not coercion. Students were empowered through trust and high expectations. A long-established honor code, joint faculty-student research projects, and twenty-four-hour access to college facilities are examples of the trust, support, and empowerment of this non-paternalistic community. Empowering and, at times, inspirationally high expectations were consistently voiced by faculty, students, and administration through rituals.

Support, challenge, and cooperation, the backbone of feminist philosophy, were a common trio of goals held by college members. Students often applaud the accomplishments of women who broke the mold, challenged stereotypes, or defied the odds concerning success in the male-dominated world. Despite the overlapping values between Mount Holyoke's goals and those of feminism, student respondents repeatedly stated that they were *not* feminists.

Supporting their point of view as nonfeminists, the political and social implications of feminism (e.g., pay equity, child care, and antiviolence) were not necessarily social issues embraced by students. Rather there was evidence that the students choose a single-sex college as an alternative to more paternalistic coeducational institutions. The oft-quoted percentage of women faculty, high achievements of graduates in nontraditional professions, and the continuing commitment to women's higher education were accepted by students as the norm. The stance was distinctly non-paternalistic but less distinctly pro-feminist.

CONCLUSION

Finally, Junior Show is most explicitly a rite of resistance (see chapter 1). This cultural performance is a parody on working hard, the single-sex environment, well-known members of the college community, and college life in general. It lampoons the very messages, including Mount Holyoke's founding values, that the students are expected to embrace most ardently.

Chapter 11

Messages, Meanings, and Root Paradigms

Culture . . . is not an abstractly ordered system based on special symbols that make it understood, but it is a product of the active members of a society who try to understand the world they live in (Orphanides, 1992, p. 110).

Rituals, a form of human action, communicate ideas and cultural meaning that are not expressed through other activities. Speaking to the most profound issues of human living (life and death, relationships, identity, integrity), rituals achieve metacommunication, express metaparadigms, and speak metacommentary (Turner, V., 1984). They voice the essence of human living and serve as a medium for social metacommentaries.

This chapter discusses the metacommunication, metaparadigms, and metacommentaries expressed through ritual forms. This synopsis takes place by exploring the messages, meanings, and metaphors of rituals.

METACOMMUNICATION

Human beings possess the cognitive ability for metacommunication, to communicate about their communication. Discussed in chapter 5 as reflexivity, this metacommunication becomes a major human meaning-making activity when provoked by rituals. Through actions, language, and behaviors that ignite metacommunication, levels upon levels of meaning and messages converge during rituals.

Through form and action engendering multiple meanings that are open to interpretation, rituals create opportunities for "multilevel communication characterized by a paradoxical structure" (Schwartzman, 1982, p. 9). These layers of meaning relate to one another and influence one another's presence. Some of the paired levels in higher education rituals include (a) obvious and hidden, (b) public and private, (c) communal and personal, (d) discursive and nondiscursive, (e) shallow and deep, and (f) single and multiple. These pairings, ends of continua, reveal the paradoxical nature of the metacommunication as well as the layers upon which the communication about the communication is built.

Communication levels in rituals can be provoked through a variety of means: multiple, conflicting messages and meanings; ingrained paradoxical metaphors; and multivocal symbols. With the varying levels of meaning in rituals, actors and participants must interpret personal meaning through a deep, inner process. Experiencing the ritual from a variety of levels, actors and participants encounter them (a) cognitively (an event like any other), (b) emotionally (linked to a uniquely personal perception), (c) spiritually (in relation to the divine and the other worldly), and (d) experientially (another human action). These myriad and often simultaneous ways of experiencing rituals add to the levels of communication or metacommunication present in rituals.

Multiple and Conflicting Ritual Messages and Meanings

Complexity is ingrained in ritual through the presence of messages and meanings. Always multiple and often conflicting, these two ritual elements represent related but distinct concepts.

Messages. A ritual's message or messages can be understood as the content deliberately built into the performance by the ritual planners (Manning, 1989a). These messages, often explicit and, at first glance, superficial, are the declared intentions of the ritual (Moore & Myerhoff, 1977). They are the ideas the planners intend to communicate through the actions and emotions of the ritual.

The explicit messages and purposes can include homecoming, recovery, chaos, pathos, religion, history of people, human condition, and commentary on the times (Morgan, 1984; Turner, V., 1977a). Ritual messages, communicated through language, action, and symbols, relate to the metacommunication possible in rituals by encompassing the "larger cultural frameworks of thought and explanation" (Moore & Myerhoff, 1977, p. 16). These "larger cultural frameworks" are the metacommunication or communication of the communication. When the ritual messages are linked to these "larger cultural frameworks," human action becomes endowed with profound meaning. In higher education, rituals are a rare opportunity to ponder, discuss, and debate the role of education in human communities, responsibilities of educated people to society, and weightiness of the "life of the mind." The presence of these messages in rituals keeps these human concerns foremost in people's realization.

With the resources of time, money, and effort invested in rituals, one might assume that a definitive purpose, at least an intended one, would be obvious. Though an observer or participant may have little difficulty identifying the "statable purpose" (Moore & Myerhoff, 1977, p. 5), building a consensus about what that purpose *truly* means can be a formidable task because the statable purpose "alludes to more than it says, and has many meanings at once" (p. 5). Ritual messages (as well as their symbols, language, and metaphors) are multivocal: they speak many truths and narrate multiple contents. Personal interpretations result in an almost endless number of theoretical explications. Despite these countless possibilities, a consensus within human communities does form. Rituals serve as a medium for that consensus and for community understanding.

Ritual Meaning. Related to but different from messages, ritual meanings are the interpretations participants construe from rituals (Manning, 1989a). Varying from person to person, interpretations and meanings attributed to rituals add to the multiple levels of metacommunication. These varying interpretations may result from, among other factors, experience with past rituals, familiarity with the ritual type, personal characteristics, and level of attentiveness. An equality of perspectives lies at the heart of these unique interpretations. The presence of multiple explanations and interpretations indicates that, indeed, "orders exist side by side" (Guba, 1985, p. 86). Rituals generate opportunities for people to ascertain personal meaning, discuss that meaning with others, and create subsequent meaning in a complex dance between self and other, inside and outside, personal and public. The paradoxes inherent in such paired opposites reflect the same paradoxes present in the metaphors so skillfully portrayed in rituals. The presence and manipulation of paradoxical ideas create a rich field on which to build meaning.

Ingrained Paradoxical Metaphors

Significant amounts of human action, rituals included, use metaphors as part of their action. Language, symbols, and actions endowed with meaning during rituals by both the planners (through messages) and the participants (through idiosyncratic meaning making) are metaphors. "Metaphor . . . is the statement of an association between things that are normally categorized in separate domains of experience. This association cannot be based on designative or literal defining features but rather on the figurative or connotative features the two things have in common" (Fernandez, 1986b, p. 176). The magic of metaphors is their ability to create spaces between the enacted half of the metaphor and its attendant meaning, the other half.

The diploma received by graduates on completion of their course requirements is an example of a metaphor in higher education. This piece of paper represents, among other ideas, the years of education the student has undergone, the status of being a college-educated adult, and the sacrifices made to obtain the degree. When a diploma symbolically stands in place of the receipt of an education, the piece of paper that is literally the diploma is one half of the metaphor. The second half, the education, completes the metaphor and enacts the meaning-making activity. Since a metaphor portrays but is *not* the concept depicted, an interpretive space is created. The metaphor halves, sometimes conflicting, often in concord, always creative, create a relationship, a gap, in between the known and unknown (Turner, V., 1974). When the known is used to discover the unknown, interpretation, learning, and development are possible. Metaphor "whose combination of familiar and unfamiliar features or unfamiliar combination of familiar features provokes us into thought, provides us with new perspectives" (p. 31). Complexity and dynamism are built into the ritual structure. Metacommunication, a building of complex ideas and levels of experience, results.

The gap in the metaphor between the literal and symbolic meanings also creates a paradox. A metaphor is simultaneously one thing *and* another. One can concurrently explore the ways that metaphor compares, contrasts, and, at times, eliminates similarities and differences. With metaphor, understanding is advanced when one comprehends how something is like something else. Paradoxical ritual metaphors were witnessed in the fusions created during the Mount Holyoke Alumnae Parade and Laurel Chain (see chapter 14). Alumnae and students, old and new, individual and group, and past and present fused during this most sentimental of rituals.

Metaphors create a larger-than-life, outside of everyday reality experience that evokes metacommunication and multiple levels of meaning. Communication is nudged to higher levels with the transcendence of the solely discursive to the symbolic, emotional, tacit, and nondiscursive.

Metaphors enacted through the actions and language of rituals allow participants to assign meaning to social behavior, conduct, and action (Turner & Turner, 1985). Culture results from the meaning-making activity of negotiating, interpreting, and experiencing metaphors. The built-in interpretive tendency of metaphor urges actors and participants to experience the ritual messages and meanings through their personal perspectives that are challenged through the metacommunicative and reflexive processes.

Metaphors are particularly effective in ritual action because they do not usually require cognition to grasp their explicit meaning. This quality allows metaphors to perform their most important work: transformation through dynamic action and language.

Transformation and Dynamism. Rituals use metaphors to effect transformations of character, social relationships, roles, and beliefs (Turner, V., 1974). The uncertainty created from the paradoxical nature of metaphors and the distance between the two meanings created an opportunity for a switch. During the ritual, the metaphor becomes enacted: this becomes that. In a moment, new roles can be imagined, new combinations joined.

> Here words prove useless, exegesis fails, and there is nothing left to do but to express a positive experience by a . . . metaphorical act—to destroy the elaborate structure one has made and admit transcendence, that is, over all that one's culture has been able to say about the experience of those who bear or have borne it to its present point of time (p. 297-298).

This transcendence, effected by the ritual experience, is a dynamic human action. One must be involved in its action, not merely a passive recipient. In fact, one can speculate that the cognitive and experiential aspects of rituals are an extremely apt form to meet the intellectual and development goals of education. Dynamism is generated through the thought and intuition needed to understand the metaphor offered during ritual. Deciphering the meaning of ritual metaphors (language, symbols, actions) is an active, engaging process.

In the ritual research conducted for this book, respondents provided testimony about the metacommunication and multiple levels of ritual meaning as they discussed their experiences with rituals. Many could tell stories about the rituals, even give detailed accounts of them without ever having attended the event being discussed. Other respondents attended the ritual and related intimate accounts from direct cultural experience. Both types of accounts clearly indicated the presence of reflexive communication about rituals.

The respondents who discussed the ritual from others' accounts (had not attended the ritual themselves) did so from a cognitive perspective. They were talking about something they understood only from secondhand description and language, not firsthand experience, feeling, and sensory perception. The latter respondents often struggled to define feelings and experiences that resided at a nondiscursive level. Metaphors enacted during rituals were understood tacitly by this latter group; they grasped the meaning at an intuitive level. The respondents knew what they knew but lacked the words to describe it. Their use of tacit knowledge, provoked by the ritual metaphors, served as a catalyst for cultural meaning making.

Metaphors fit ritual action because they are inherently dynamic. Their dynamism emerges from the fusion of two symbols, ideas, or meanings (in the diploma example, a piece of paper and an educated person). Because a relationship can be drawn between the two meanings, one idea can be substituted for the other (Turner, V., 1974). Each idea represented by the metaphor has at least two, and usually countless, meanings. Cultural knowledge expands with the presence of combinations and interpretations. "Components of one system [one half of the metaphor] enter into dynamic relations with components of the other" (p. 29).

Multivocal Symbols

Symbols are ritual elements packed with multiple meanings (Turner, V., 1977a), multivocality, and ambiguity. In addition to metaphors, language, and actions, rituals communicate their messages and meaning through symbols. Uniquely able to limit and expand personal and communal meaning, symbols adapt to a variety of purposes and meanings. Symbols can be objects, activities, relationships, words, gestures, or spatial arrangements. Regardless of their form, ritual symbols are often "dense, multilayered expressions with both cognitive and affective dimensions" irreducible "to any single level of meaning" (Oring, 1993, p. 276). Their multivocality enables them to condense multiple ideas, relations, and actions. Paradoxical, conflicting, and dynamic ideas can be represented simultaneously (Turner, V., 1977a).

Symbols are used effectively in rituals when they relate to the belief structure of the community and are closely linked to the larger social structure. Symbols add to the complexity and dynamism of ritual metacommunication in the way they complicate the messages and meanings of the event, enrich community meaning, and spark culture building. They "carry implicit messages, distinguishable from the overt ingredients intended by the designers of a ritual; they are part of its creation but not clearly planned or controlled. When they are well chosen and understood, they do their work unnoticed" (Myerhoff, 1984, p. 160).

A potent symbol in the Mount Holyoke College ritual study was the laurel woven into a chain for the Alumnae Parade. Laurel has long carried meaning as a symbol for honor and glory. At Mount Holyoke College, the laurel carried by the graduating seniors in years past was picked from nearby woods and woven by the students. With a decline in wild laurel, the modern-day chain was assembled by a professional florist. But, meaningfully over the years, the laurel came to carry many messages: a medium for a Vietnam War protest effort for seniors in the 1960s, victory over a less-than-welcoming environment for students of color, environmental activism, and reflection of the college's beauty (Manning, 1989a). These meanings are known and unknown, public and personal, cognitive and experiential. As such, many meanings enacted across the years by various ritual actors go unnoticed.

Because the work of symbols is "unnoticed" publicly, ritual symbols provide a rich store of material for discussion, exegesis, and metacommentary. Their multiple meanings, purposefully distorted and often incomplete, provide rich material for pre- and post-ritual storytelling.

Symbols and Higher Education. Symbols make use of an inexhaustible range of referents (Myerhoff, 1984). Whether flags sporting school colors, street signs with institutional logos, or memorabilia adorned with the campus mascot, symbols have a long history in higher education (Lederman, 1993; Shea, 1993).

School colors, among other meanings, can convey campus unity, sports team fanaticism, and institutional affiliation. The buildings of New York University (NYU), in the heart of New York City's Greenwich Village, nondescriptively blend into the mix of city buildings. Urban campuses, evolving over time through the purchase of noncontiguous properties, are frequently strewn across numerous blocks. To convey a sense of place and unified appearance, NYU distinguished their buildings with purple school color flags. One need merely glance down a street to recognize the presence of this urban university.

As multivocal metaphors, symbols point to more than one image. The multiplicity of meanings, levels of communication, and complexity of metaphors and symbols inherent in rituals allow these cultural activities to construct larger images, metaparadigms, of meaning and experience. "In requiring enactments involving symbols, it bids us to participate in its messages, even enacting meanings we cannot conceive or believe" (Myerhoff, 1984, p. 151). Using intuition, ritual participants can discern meanings leading to a renewed vision of self, achievement, or community.

METAPARADIGMS

Metaparadigms, also called root paradigms, "serve as culturally induced scripts" (McLaren, 1986, p. 134). They are often expressed as axiomatic rules, prevailing motifs, basic definitions of culture, and paradigmatic myths of a community, society, or institution (McLaren; Turner & Turner, 1985). Exposed during rituals, root paradigms express the ideals of the community, all that is sacred within the culture. Ritual work makes visible, even if momentarily, an ideology or basic model (Moore & Myerhoff, 1977).

Particularly when enacted in everyday places, the performance of rituals carries underlying community assumptions, past history, and collective meaning into present reality (Flanigan, 1990). Ordinary selves, routine time, and banal images are fused with larger cultural scripts. The everyday becomes transcendent. The transcendent becomes everyday. "Root paradigms . . . . go beyond the cognitive and even the moral to the existential domain, and in so doing become clothed with allusiveness, implicitness, and metaphor" (Turner, V., 1974, p. 64).

Through the expression of metaparadigms, which can be sacred, ritual action invites humans to endow their lives with meaning, to transcend ordinary individual concerns. Because root paradigms involve issues beyond the mundane, they express a moral and ethical context. Right and wrong in the context of that community can be expressed in ritual and held open to examination. People are presented with role-modeled images and behavior upon which to base their actions. Rituals give root paradigms form and visibility enacting the deep-seated meanings of a culture.

Root Paradigms and Crises

Victor Turner (1974, 1977a; Turner & Turner, 1985) speculated that crisis was a particularly ripe occasion for the expression of the fundamental roots of a community. Theorizing about a ritual form he called social dramas, Turner identified four stages: breach, crisis, redressive action, and reintegration. When a community is in crisis, social dramas allow for the expression of root paradigms, the resolution of ideals that no longer meet the needs of the community, and the creation of a new belief or set of beliefs that better fit the redressive action needed to resolve the crisis situation. During times of crisis (student deaths, campus tragedy), "communitas emerges from its small enclaves into public space" (Turner, V., 1972, p. 289).

An example of a crisis in higher education requiring a social drama to resolve the situation is a sudden or long-term lack of presidential leadership. The very foundation of a college or university can be affected as mission and purpose erode, management fragments, and the community loses coherence. The institution is well served by a presidential inauguration, which is a celebration and occasion to welcome a new member into the community but is also an opportunity for redressive action regarding the languishing leadership. The basis for the community and institutional raison d'etre is addressed in a ritual that can narrate fundamental root paradigms and ideals.

Rituals as social dramas within higher education can achieve this redressive effect in several ways. These include (a) refocusing the crisis by offering alternative dominant themes within the ritual; (b) reinterpreting history through the ritual's messages; (c) projecting a redefined, more optimistic future; (d) allowing time and opportunity for cathartic expression; and (e) resealing and reinforcing the community beliefs in question.

In the first case, sleight of hand during the ritual shifts attention from the crisis to the ritual theme. In the second case, history is reinterpreted; the terms of the crisis are given a more promising spin. The third case has ritual planners and participants engendering hope through the verbal and symbolic promises of a brighter future. In the fourth case, the crisis is exposed during ritual, giving the community an opportunity for comment. The ritual becomes a cathartic social drama during which fundamental institutional values are expressed. Community members can vocalize their joy and rage in an effort to address shaken community values and beliefs. The final means for redress often used in higher education is to didactically remind participants of the community's values. The effort here is to remind people that, despite the temporary breach, the values still hold. The case study in this book depicting a convocation ritual is a good example of this type of ritual purpose. Because the college experienced several racial incidents, the ritual planners addressed the crisis by selecting diversity as a theme against which they could express fundamental institutional values (service, achievement, and leadership).

The problem with these redressive approaches to a temporary social crisis is "that the more persuasive the root metaphor or archetype, the more chance it has of becoming a self-certifying myth, sealed off from empirical disproof" (Turner, V., 1974, p. 29). In other words, the unreal can become, very convincingly, the real. Root paradigms, arising from social crises, must be chosen very carefully (Turner, V.) because of their propensity to make the unreal real and vice versa. Root paradigms speak to the very heart of the community, its most fervent beliefs and ideals. The wrong choice, institutionalized and repeatedly enacted, can become part of the institutional culture.

Root Paradigms and Higher Education

Similar to other institutions, cultures, and communities, higher education contains root paradigms that underscore the messages of campus rituals. These root paradigms are the substance from which ritual messages are constructed and meanings construed. Several prominent higher education root paradigms include teaching, research, and service; institutional authority; student resistance (including reversals and inversions); intellectual achievement; a community of scholars; and academic honesty. Root paradigms often become visible in local missions such as religious affiliation, research or knowledge discovery, and community service.

At Mount Holyoke College, the rituals research discussed in this book uncovered correspondences between ritual symbols, root paradigm belief systems, and the social context. An emphasis on nature and peace of mind was mirrored in the specially built amphitheater. This outdoor site was built to accommodate rituals such as graduation and convocation. The importance of physical and mental health was reiterated in rituals such as Mountain Day. Service and relationships to larger purposes were epitomized in Baccalaureate. The sacredness of a service mission was reinforced by enactment of rituals in the college chapel.

Root paradigms, particularly when expressed in rituals, possess the dual function of creating and shaping meaning. Root paradigms come into being through human imagination, consensus, and human action. They are not "natural" (derived externally from nature or handed down by God) but, rather, are a human-derived activity. Likewise, they are shaped by the cultural action of rituals. The meaning of root paradigms drifts or can change abruptly with time and differing enactments.

Mythical Paradigms

The foundational level at which root paradigms are expressed, the fundamental issues they address, and the drama of their form endows them with powerful persuasiveness. People come to believe the messages communicated during rituals.

Made-Up-Ness. Root paradigms can be thought of as "canonized magic" (Flanigan, 1990, p.51). The "made-up-ness" of reality, a product of human imagination, is canonized or made official in rituals, ceremonies, and cultural performances. Fiction becomes reality often to such a degree that the "truth" of the root paradigm is indisputable.

There is a sense of unquestionability (McLaren, 1986) about rituals. This unquestionability is communicated through a created perception that urges the participants to believe that what is being presented is true, no matter how divorced from reality. Although McLaren was discussing the unquestionability of ritualized classroom content, method of instruction, and authority, there exists an unquestionability about the content of the rituals interpreted in this book. Ritual planners use this form as a way to persuade students and other community members about what is true. This process is not without danger as one cannot convince skeptical, intelligent students to give up their right to question some of what is "given" as truth during rituals. The students are too smart and the content is too rich for the ritual messages to be accepted as truth without discussion or dialogue.

Rituals "make assertions, claims that are at the same time denials of unacceptable realities" (Myerhoff, 1977, p. 214). Administrators and faculty can claim that the college is of higher quality and more challenging academically than the facts support. An institution could, by all evidence, be failing financially and experiencing enrollment declines but believe it will survive. This "fiction," repeated and reinforced in rituals, can gather enough strength to become reality.

In the 1990s, higher education experienced a crisis of public confidence. One can interpret this situation as involving the presence of a fictional metaparadigm, or overriding belief, concerning the importance of a college education. The evidence that the public no longer supports, without question, the value of higher education has had little impact on this internal belief.

The made-up-ness of culture and its interplay with root paradigms and ritual action is an essential human activity. Without forms like ritual to give culture its "concreteness," the "made-up-ness" of culture (including basic beliefs, root paradigms, and prescribed behaviors) would be evident. In fact, when rituals fail (symbols misfire, messages are too incongruent with lived realities), "we may glimpse their basic artifice, and from this apprehend the fiction and invention underlying all culture" (Myerhoff, 1984, p. 152).

By going through the motions, accepting ritual meaning as truth, following those who lead, participants accept the "truth" of the ritual. The fact that those truths are, at best, "made up" and, therefore, pliable is not only ignored but of little consequence. The myopia of internal yet fictional or mythical root paradigms is a dangerous and powerful consequence of socially constructed reality.

Missing Root Paradigms

As one examines the metaparadigms within higher education (teaching, research, and service; academic honesty), the root paradigms that are missing are revealing. Several root paradigms conspicuous by their absence include kindness, civility, temperance, and balance.

METACOMMENTARY

Ultimately, the evocative and cognitive reactions to a ritual can be experienced at a metacommentary level. Participants' past experiences, cultural knowledge, and community beliefs are folded into an interpretation drawn from the experiences of the event. The experience is acquired at many different levels so that commentary on top of commentary is effected. The ritual, in this way, can serve as a metacommentary through exegesis and consensus.

Exegesis

. Through storytelling and mythmaking, a ritual can adopt a vastly different character from that originally intended. Before, during, and after a ritual, "exegetical meaning . . . the commentary accompanying a ritual" (Grimes, 1990, p. 144) occurs. This exegetical conversation, expanding the messages and meanings of the ritual, is an essential part of its action. Preceding and following the event, its meaning is discussed, made sense of, thought through, and analyzed.

Ritual participants, through the critical explanation and analysis of an exegesis, expand and interpret the event's messages and meanings and create new cultural knowledge (Goody, 1977). Similar to the structure and antistructure dynamic discussed by Victor Turner (see chapter 7), the exegetical storytelling releases ritual from a static form—one that never changes—and transforms it into a living entity. Accounts of the ritual and its possible meanings expand through conversations as participants and nonparticipants work through the messages they witnessed and meanings they constructed.

Telling old ritual stories and creating new ones is part of ritual action. These stories and the accompanying exegetical commentary are passed down through time (Oring, 1993). Interpretations grow through this meaning-making conversation long after the ritual has ended. Through an exegesis, the stature and importance of the event is magnified, messages and meanings spread from ritual witnesses to non-attenders, and the ritual conveys and shapes meaning in the community beyond the action of its original enactment. "When it loses its capacity to play with ideas, symbols, and meanings, when it loses its cultural evolutionary resilience, ritual ceases to be an effective metalanguage or an agent of collective reflexivity" (Turner & Turner, 1985, p. 165).

Consensus

The ritual process, including the performance, history, myths, storytelling, and exegesis, constitutes a consensus seeking process for the community. A communal consensus can build around the ideals, purposes, and expectations of community life as expressed in the metaparadigms of rituals. Despite the interpretation, multivocality of symbols, and multiple realities and meanings offered during ritual, these events align people toward a common consensus. Consistent form, repeated process, and traditional language and methods combine to create a consensus across time.

These events evoke emotions about community "truths." People attend rituals, experience a communal recitation of past and present beliefs, synchronize their movements in a gesture of group cooperation, and temporarily relinquish their individuality in order to be and act as part of a group (Burns & Laughlin, 1979). From this perspective, rituals are a search to discover commonalities with the people with whom one lives (Kapferer, 1984).

In a positive sense, the order offered by rituals provides a model upon which to base and synchronize behavior with others. In light of the complexities of choices and individual interpretation involved in living in social communities, "collective ritual can be seen as an especially dramatic attempt to bring some particular part of life firmly and definitely into orderly control" (Moore & Myerhoff, 1977, p. 3). Without this consensus and order, community life would be chaotic, language would be impossible, and common ground upon which to speak and act would be nonexistent. Without reflection on identity, discussion about purpose, and recognition of accomplishments, community members would be bereft of models upon which to form their identities.

In a negative sense, rituals can exert undue control over an individual's creativity and personal choice. In light of the complexity of everyday living, rituals can act as an assurance that there is order and control. Rituals present a contrived order to the chaos of individual interpretations and myriad of personal choices. In this sense, rituals are dangerous in the manner in which they limit an individual's choice and offer models for living, thinking, and acting.

Without the consensus fashioned by rituals and other cultural events, the cultural life of institutions and communities would disintegrate. Members would struggle to create meaning over and over without the repetitive action and language of rituals. Despair, confusion, lack of community, and chaos could result (Orphanides, 1992).

SUMMARY

Rituals possess the ability to enable participants to collect cultural knowledge in a cumulative manner. Through an exegesis, attendance at some, but not necessarily all, rituals, and simply living in the college community, a student reaches the end of his or her college years with a vast store of accumulated knowledge. Because they learn tacitly, people are hard-pressed to reconstruct the accumulation of this knowledge. How could a student, without ever having attended a specific ritual, know precisely how to behave? How was the knowledge embodied in ritual messages incorporated into the individual's history? Even without an explicit idea of the process by which it works, the accumulation of cultural knowledge is inevitable.

Chapter 12

Mary Lyon's Birthday Celebration

"We all know why we're here."

—Alumna panel moderator and former
director of observances

Mary Lyon's Birthday and Alumnae Awards celebration tended to be a quiet, low-key internal ritual consisting of a panel discussion in the student center and an invitation-only dinner. The only aspect of the event visible to undergraduates was the annual appearance of Deacon Porter's Hat, a steamed pudding and hard sauce dessert. Student respondents commented that the sight of the dessert was hardly cause for celebration. A senior respondent commented that the dessert was, "disgusting—I don't know why they serve it. I don't know what it is—this brown bread with this glob of cream cheese."

This year's awards celebrated the one hundred ninetieth anniversary of Mary Lyon's birth. To honor the founder, the alumnae bestowed awards on recent graduates at this annual celebration and dinner. The student newspaper described the birthday tradition as a time to honor "recipients of the award . . . chosen on their demonstration of achievement in their lives, professions, or communities consistent with the humane values Mary Lyon exemplified in her life and inspired in others."

THE PANEL

The alumnae award recipients settled in their seats at the front of the room in the student center. Women old and young, fulfilling different roles at the college, sat in the audience and reflected on how the college changed their lives. The ritual's organizers were adamant that undergraduates attend the Mary Lyon Awards. The students were future award recipients; their presence was vital as the current award recipients role-modeled excellence, achievement, and leadership.

The Mary Lyon Awards Committee chose the award recipients from among a wide range of alumnae candidates with equally impressive records of excellence in professional, family, and community life. Achievements such as the ones being honored during the ritual were expected at the college. The faculty referred to

Mount Holyoke women as the "cream of the cream of American women"— praise that respondents felt would not be delivered at a coeducational college.

Students, alumnae, faculty, and others recognized that the college's activities, including this dinner and awards ritual, were driven by the underlying, ideological structure. This ideology made a difference in the education provided. The ever present academic and personal support, number of tenured female faculty, and high expectations for success were a few elements of that ideology. The award recipients commented on this phenomenon with the belief that in coeducational environments, "women were given equal opportunity, but they are not always given every opportunity."

Although the mission and purpose of women's higher education was clearly feminist, the vision of the college was conceived and established long before feminism was in vogue. Despite its historical ties to educational access efforts for women, few current students, particularly when discussing the single-sex nature of the college, mentioned feminism. One senior respondent went so far as to say, "I don't consider myself a big feminist. I'm a humanist." This humanism was expressed as opportunity, freedom, and empowerment.

Rather than feminist ideals, students and alumnae attributed their choice to attend Mount Holyoke to their desire for the highest quality education, engaged leadership opportunities, and the highest standard of achievement. An alumna panelist said, "The change today is that women can make a choice." At this college, students' work is not judged by what many at the college viewed as a biased, paternalistic standard. The barriers of this standard (competition, aggressiveness, and detachment) were transformed to egalitarianism, empowerment, and support.

"Being here had a tremendous impact on the direction my life took"; "You can do whatever you want to and do it well" were comments shared by the young alumnae award recipients. The ideals of service, excellence, achievement, and pride dominated the conversation among the panelists. The women in the audience, many of them alumnae themselves, were also invited to share their thoughts about Mary Lyon's ideals and their college experience. Undergraduates quieted their usually gregarious selves and listened attentively to their forerunners' accomplishments.

Words flowed among the award recipients as they discussed ability and success. "We did everything here." They learned leadership, equality, and the importance of sticking up for other people. There was a "confidence that you can develop in a single-sex situation." Mount Holyoke College "provides us with endless opportunities to . . . make a significant contribution in whatever endeavor we choose to undertake." Panelists and audience members expressed pride, commitment, renewal, and connection to others.

The stories of the younger alumnae award recipients reinforced the college's ideals: cheerleading from professors; nonexistent barriers to leadership positions; challenges of this special environment; the field wide open for success, achievement, and learning. Students were resolutely supported in their desire to pursue positions from which they might otherwise have backed away. At Mount Holyoke, said the panelists, there was the "opportunity to become a student in depth." Students could thrive in an environment where challenge was coupled with constant encouragement.

This combination spurred them on to high achievement. This institutionalized sentiment was announced in an admissions brochure so that prospective students received the message. "What truly defines Mount Holyoke is its unique place as a college for women. Women count. Women are noticed. Women are listened to. Women are respected. At Mount Holyoke there are no assumptions or stereotypes. Nobody's on the sidelines."

The three alumnae honored with the Founder's Award were exemplars of how women developed as a result of their experiences at the college. They do not arrive on campus as fully formed, successful women. What was important was how the students fulfilled their potential. The process started with a student who was gently and purposefully encouraged and empowered to grow into her own person.

Mount Holyoke was a place where freedom existed for a woman to become her best. One could see who she was, how she contributed, and how she became a leader. The junior class president described the college as "that place where we open new doors and set foot into areas which we never before envisioned ourselves." The dean of students said that the "opportunity for bright, highly motivated, interesting, lively women to work and live together for four years, devoted to expanding their thoughts, their visions, and their outlooks is an opportunity that must be cherished." Working and living together at Mount Holyoke might be the first time they would live in a single-sex, supportive environment. A "community of women who live and work and lead each other is very exciting."

The alumnae honored were among the many at the college who learned to be critical thinkers and leaders in professions often dominated by men. The college had affected their lives and they, in turn, made a difference in their professions. "Just the presence of women in professions that are traditionally male makes a difference." They were willing to sacrifice, add on, and accept new personal and professional challenges because they "could never quit" their professions—the ministry, symphony orchestra musician, and medicine—which they worked so hard to enter.

THE DINNER

On- and off-campus guests walked from the student center room and panel to the college's conference center and dinner celebration. Lights from the dining room reflected in the adjacent pond where water hesitated before cascading over a dam spanned by a wooden bridge. The walk to dinner took one past a small building, called the pump house. The modern conference center, built on the hill next to the pond, contrasted in age and design to the grey-shingled pump house. Certainly not fulfilling any current purpose, the structure stood as testimony to the days when water was pumped up from the lakes to the hilltop dormitories. The small wooden house, identified by a bronze plaque as the oldest structure on campus, was the only remaining proof of Mount Holyoke's original buildings. The campus was ravaged by the 1896 fire, one of many in the college's history. The community took advantage of each tragic fire to rebuild the campus in a Phoenix-like manner.

Flowers, china, and well-placed hors d'oeuvres filled the coffee and end tables of the conference center living room. The planning committee assigned the seating for the invitation-only dinner by generations. Older alumnae sat among undergraduates with a range of ages filling the intervening years. With this cast of characters in place, the dinner conversation turned to a familiar topic of discussion: whether the founder was *actually* buried in the grave that crowned the college's grove. Some people asserted that the founder's resting place was not at Mount Holyoke, despite the wrought iron fence and the marked grave but at another college whose founding she aided. Or perhaps she was, as many believed, buried in her hometown. Pictures of her funeral held at the college did not convince the skeptics. It was rumored that she *had* been buried at Mount Holyoke then exhumed and moved to another grave site.

One alumnae dinner guest insisted that the story be set straight. The truth of Mary Lyon's burial was an important issue for people who believed the meanings conveyed in the college's rituals. As a spirit very much alive on campus and an ideal upon which the college was founded, Mary Lyon's physical presence on campus was vital to the perpetuation of these underlying, foundational beliefs. Events like Founder's Day and the Laurel Chain, actually held at the grave, would seem less genuine without the founder's physical presence. The truth spoken in rituals would surely be called into question by participants if the grave around which these rituals occurred was empty. Despite the issues and beliefs at stake, the presence of Mary Lyon in her campus grave was a prevalent campus myth. Any resolution was unlikely; the controversy raged on.

Protests continued over coffee not just about the founder's grave but the well-publicized claim that the college was the oldest women's college in America. Mary Lyon established or assisted with the establishment of another college that also claimed the honored title of "oldest." Supporters asserted that Mount Holyoke was actually the oldest college because a collegiate curriculum was taught there first. This was, by their claims, the original institution of higher education for women.

The single-sex status of the college was another topic of hot debate and dinner conversation. The argument entailed whether the institution should remain single sex or turn coeducational as so many sister schools had. A trustee speaking via a student newspaper interview said that a

> first rate women's college has got to hang in there because the questions that are faced by the feminist movement have not by any means been resolved to the point where we have gained equity on all fronts: salary scales, access. When that happens then you can say, "Maybe the job of the women's college is really finished." But I think there's so much that has to be solved and that has to be solved by self-confident, able, well-trained women.

Many people on campus including the current president claimed that, if need be, this would be the last single-sex institution.

The Deacon Porter's Hat arrived as expected. Already apportioned into round servings, the dessert did not resemble the college benefactor's infamous stovepipe hat. The students were correct in their assessment—the dessert was unpleasant. But as a tradition dating back to the founder's days, the annual appearance of the "treat" continued.

HONORING THE FOUNDER

The founder "would have liked this," said an alumna from the Class of '51 who addressed the dinner guests. "This" referred to something different than the candlelit tables, rich food, and trappings of the modern conference center. That finery might even have offended Mary Lyon's evangelical tastes. The wine on the tables would certainly not have been allowed during her time as the college's president. But Mary Lyon "would have liked" the fact that students, alumnae, and administrators came together to honor achievement and excellence. These ideals upon which she based her life—using one's talents, achieving success, fulfilling the responsibility of service, and returning something to the college through the work one does—she also built into the fabric of the college. Those ideals were reflected in the work and the words of the alumnae honored with the award named in her honor.

Citations read as part of the after-dinner program celebrated the excellence of the three award recipients. They were truly exceptional: a musician and mother who believed that one could not have it all without sacrifice, a doctor and researcher who struggled through physical pain to become one of the youngest administrators at her hospital, and a minister and community leader who attributed her spiritual development directly to the college. Their actions reflected Mary Lyon's words: "Go where no one else will go—do what no one else will do."

The alumnae and students shared dinner, campus myths, and stories of their experiences, old and new. By participating in the ritual of achievement being enacted, the standard bearers and future caretakers of the college's ideals were respectively honored and groomed. The youngest generation of rising alumnae were shown their place in perpetuating the ideals and living through the college's traditions. The strong commitment to the college and its ideals was carefully nurtured, transmitted, and tended.

PATTERNS AND THEMES

Mary Lyon's Birthday Celebration created a space and time to express several themes within the campus community: unwavering spirit, meaning making, and multivocality.

"Unwavering" Spirit

Mary Lyon's Birthday Celebration defined and perpetuated a unique Mount Holyoke sense of spirit, described by a Class of '21 respondent as "unwavering." Throughout the research on rituals at Mount Holyoke College, the word "spirit" was seen in rituals to connote the college's founding ideals, the attitude the founder endowed to the community, and the unique resilience and tenaciousness of the community. The rituals and traditions were essential to the college's spirit. They communicated and transformed this spirit. As expressed by Moore and Myerhoff (1977), the rituals both perpetuated *and* created culture. The spirit of the place was an essential aspect of that culture.

The traditions discussed during Mary Lyon's Birthday celebration (experiences of the honorees as undergraduates, standards for scholarship, and opportunities for achievement) were evidence to reinforce and justify the students' and alumnae's belief in Mount Holyoke. The ritual was a living enactment of the beliefs of the college and its members. Through it, the college participants created time and opportunity for students and alumnae to express and build an emotional attachment to the college.

Through ritual, the women of the college could gather as a group, collectively recite and hear the community-held beliefs, and grow closer to one another through their shared experiences. When a college community's survival is threatened by budget cuts, decreased enrollment, or other foreseen and unforeseen events, colleges are forced to make choices about their identity. Threatened communities (e.g., financially unstable institutions, colleges facing an unwanted change in mission) often make one of two choices: they continue on the course set by their founding mission or they transform that mission. At Mount Holyoke, a college determined to maintain its founding mission, the rituals were an opportunity to express their common beliefs, commit to those values, and buttress their shared purposes.

Meaning Making

The commonality of shared purposes and beliefs, whether under adverse or positive conditions, assures the community that their work has meaning. Through ritual, participants verbalize their purposes and shared beliefs, make those beliefs available for confirmation and critique, and convince themselves and each other that their lives have meaning. Perhaps there is no coincidence between the prevalence of rituals on college campuses and the nature of higher education outcomes that are abstract, intellectually driven and hard to define. However, the rituals, particularly coupled with the assurances of a rich, established history, secure the perpetuation of the community and the individual. As such, voicing the college's legacy through individual actions of alumnae is a potent survival strategy. The communication of the college's mission with its attendant messages of quality, achievement, and service assumes a moral imperative. The maintenance of the spirit of the place is essential to preserving a distinctive, high quality sense of self among the participants.

Multivocality

The panel discussion, dinner, and awards ceremony in honor of Mary Lyon's birthday vividly expressed the ideals of community espoused by the college's members. The speeches and presence of generations of alumnae and students revealed the continuity and perpetuation of the founding ideals. These founding ideals were expressed through symbols and words that conveyed the multivocal nature of ritual. That is, the panelists' testimony could be interpreted in multiple ways by people in the audience. Each person shaped her personal meaning from the participants' words and interpreted her experiences through the shared stories and accounts of the panelists.

Multivocality was illustrated by using the espoused ideals of the college. The founding ideal of service was met and addressed by each of the honorees at the Founder's Awards in different ways: service to God, service to family, and service to a profession. The ideal of community was expressed in terms of college, local, and worldwide communities. Each woman expressed her interpretation of the founding ideals (community, service, social justice, and achievement) in a different way. Their words expressed multiple ways of interpreting those underlying college ideals.

CONCLUSIONS

The Mary Lyon Awards and Birthday Celebration acted as a homecoming celebration for the honored alumnae, an expression of pride for attending alumnae, and a rite of integration for undergraduate students. The multiplicity of its purposes and multivocality of its messages simultaneously attested to the complexity of life on campus and strength of the commitment to the founder's ideals.

Chapter 13

Old Traditions in New Places: The Oxymoron of "New" Rituals

Perhaps the genre's survival and power, and the continued vitality of its ethos, are signs of something deep in human nature (Raybin, 1990, p. 38).

RITUALS AND CAMPUS CULTURES

There is little doubt that campus rituals, ceremonies, and cultural performances are a major source of campus culture (Manning, 1994a; 1994b). Despite the fact that traditions are commonplace at many institutions, administrators, faculty, and students often attribute a lack of school spirit to insufficient numbers of "traditions." Something is missing, an emptiness or lack of culture, in institutions devoid of rituals or where these events have grown stale. It is not only the ritual action that is missed but the beliefs, principles, and even feelings engendered.

Perhaps most important, rituals mask arbitrariness (McLaren, 1986). They make us believe that there is order and logic behind the made-up reality being expressed in ritual and enacted in everyday life. The form of the ritual, including repetition (Giddens, 1979), evocativeness (Moore & Myerhoff, 1977), liminality (Turner, V., 1969), communitas (Turner, V., 1974), and exegesis (Grimes, 1990) lend a more-real-than-real feeling to rituals.

Rituals express ideas difficult to communicate or engender in other ways. These beliefs, foundational to the very nature of the college, are sacred. Rituals become a place and time to express, reiterate, and even transform these beliefs. Ideas expressed in higher education rituals include identity, community, leadership, and centeredness.

Individual and Community Identity Building

Individual Identity. A major activity for students during the college years is identity formation. Whether they are striking out on their own, choosing a career, considering choices about sexuality, or engaging in the many developmental tasks undertaken in college, forming an individual identity is a major college activity (Chickering & Reisser, 1991). As is wellknown, psychosocial developmental is accompanied by cognitive and moral development during the college years (Astin, 1993; Baxter Magolda, 1992; Gilligan, 1982; Pascarella & Terenzini, 1991; Perry, 1970). Higher education administrators and faculty diligently attempt to foster critical thinking, sharpen cognitive abilities, and urge ethical decision making.

Community Identity. In addition to the individual identity development fostered during the college years, group and/or institutional identity development is also nurtured. Students, perhaps for the first time in their lives, identify closely with an institution. In a process beginning with college admissions and progressing well past graduation, the college or university from which the degree is obtained becomes an alma mater. The student identifies with the institution (often through accoutrements of dress and paraphernalia announcing his or her college affiliation) and other college members.

Whether at an individual or community level, a student's value system is often shaken during college. He or she is asked to associate with the college's belief system, challenged by meeting diverse peers, and perhaps asked to defend the belief system he or she merely inherited from his or her parents. Identity, with the institution or as an individual self, is particularly challenged during ritual. One is asked to stand with and for the institution, to proclaim him or herself as a community member, to exercise leadership talents, and to adhere to the community belief structure. Through a paradoxical performance of individuality and conformity, beliefs are made visible through rituals. Students are asked to rely on their individual strength and sense of self while meeting an institutionally determined set of challenges. In some rituals such as graduation, participants are ironically asked to dress alike (academic regalia) and to embark on the most individualistic journey of their lives (commencement).

Ideological principles conflicting with the college's founding beliefs can be denied during ritual (Oring, 1993). Ritual is a stage upon which ideas conflicting with the belief structure can be denied while the ideals acceptable to the community are lauded. The conflicting ideas are suppressed "to promote the celebration of certain principles upon which the integration of society depends" (p. 286). In this way, ritual action works as a social control device convincing participants that all is well. At least on the surface, one is convinced of the widespread consensus concerning the underlying ideals. This ritual dynamic explains why certain ideas (e.g., patriarchy, a less prominent place for women in society, racist ideology, hierarchical power relationships), no longer palatable to many, continue.

I Becomes We. Despite the communication of unpalatable ideas and time-weary beliefs, humans are inherently drawn to rituals as they link the individual to the group. Ritual allows humans to balance individual and communal selves. The "I" becomes "we" as the individual allows him or herself to be led within the context of the ritual form. Individual and group fuse through shared saga and myth, joint celebrations of individual accomplishments, and vivid presentations of communal actions. During rituals, individual history fuses with group history to become part of the community ethos.

Individual and communal histories intertwine until it is difficult to determine where stories begin and end, who the original author was, and what the initial story entailed. During rituals there is often a moment or period of time when individual and group action are so fused that it is impossible to tell where one ends and the other begins. Rituals offer a means through which communal actions, stories, and beliefs can be formed, perpetuated, and shared as one entity.

Rituals allow people to connect to entities larger than their individual selves. Rituals become essential to college communities because the dynamic of merging the self to a community occurs in few other circumstances. Students link to alumni, the institution, faculty, and administrators. Alumni connect with the institution as well as their past and future selves through the rituals and ceremonies of homecoming.

> The convincing form and persuasive style of ceremonies create opportunities for
> . . . [college members] to venture beyond their individual needs and commit to the
> values and ideals of the community. Ceremonies and rituals link us to other people.
> The statements of "who we are as a community," "what our goals are as a college,"
> and "what we feel is important" connect students, faculty, and administrators to a
> community of friends, scholars, and colleagues (Manning, 1989a, p. 61).

Building community through rituals, often the raison d'etre of culture building activities, has no substitute. "To abandon [rituals] . . . would be painfully self-alienating" (Rappaport, 1992, p. 18). To discontinue ritual practices on college campuses could precipitate a lonely, autonomous existence, communally and individually.

The ramifications of shared communal and individual action are significant. While these moments of fusion of individual and community histories are clearly evident on ritual-laden campuses, institutions nearly devoid of rituals also undertake culture-building activities that link individual and communal purposes. Whether through rituals, story-telling, or other cultural ways of being within a community, people who work, live, and study on college campuses find ways to build shared purposes, values, and beliefs.

Mutual Engagement. The multivocal character of rituals and their symbols creates opportunities for all voices, including those different from the norm, to be present in the culture. If the ritual is built with sincerity, emphasizes active rather than passive responses, and embodies the courage necessary to explore the deeper issues within human living, ritual actors and participants engage each other in meaningful action. Through rituals, humans can challenge one another, role-model ideals beyond their individual imaginations, and exceed personal expectations.

Leadership

On college campuses, leadership is taught, modeled, and encouraged through a variety of means. Societal expectations dictate that higher education institutions prepare people for leadership in, among other settings, corporations, government, and education. Rituals are a time, place, and opportunity to teach leadership. Administration of rituals, ceremonies, and cultural performances are opportunities to teach leadership. Amassing an audience, arranging ceremonial logistics, and executing a large-scale event build the leadership skills of organization and planning.

Award ceremonies, convocations, and graduations often evoke emotion-laden language to communicate leadership principles: responsibility to community, importance of education, courage to cultivate vision. Ritual emotion, messages, and language converge to communicate the principle that the leadership encouraged and modeled is crucial to communal and individual survival.

Confusion and Paradox. The meaning-making capacity of rituals is another means used by alumni, administration, faculty, and students to teach leadership. Specifically, leadership is taught during rituals through the contradictions and paradoxes built into the action. Independence, self-reliance, and critical thinking are encouraged through unexplained confusion and unresolved paradoxes proffered during rituals (Manning, 1989a). Confusion and paradox can be employed to teach initiative and responsibility. When messages are purposely vague and even mystifying, students have to dig within their imagination for an explanation. This creativity and the confidence it ultimately builds fold directly into leadership skills.

Stewardship. An aspect of leadership deeply embedded in ritual action is stewardship. Ritual action transfers the college's belief structure from present generations of students to future ones. Because rituals are performed communally, the beliefs are not simply housed within individuals. Ritual action is not simply a matter of passing the beliefs from one person to the next. While some ritual actors such as presidents and pivotal characters may symbolically represent the institution, founding values are actually held communally as well as individually through the public practice of the ritual. Founding beliefs, through ritual action, are held in trust by the institution's leaders in the name of the entire community. One can concretely see the institution's beliefs being honorifically bestowed on the steward during rituals such as presidential inaugurations. The new president actually wears the symbols (e.g., college seal) representing the institution's beliefs. Charters are passed from old to new president for safekeeping. The evocative language and music of ritual convey to these past, present, and future leaders that the stewardship bestowed on them is a sacred honor.

Centeredness

Individual and community identity development, leadership cultivation, and stewardship of the institution's values add to the college's capacity to hold a center. In a poetic sense, having a center means that the college possesses beliefs of value to the world. The work in educating students, discovering and generating knowledge, and contributing to the respective communities is essential and meaningful. For an institution to possess such meaning is to be centered.

Colleges in want of a firm belief structure or structure of founding values lack a center. Without the coherence of the founding beliefs, faculty, administrators, and students flail in various, often opposing, directions. There are insufficient communal values to pull the various members from their individual tasks. Little to nothing pulls them together as a group. Community identity is missing or unclear because they lack the centeredness upon which a strong sense of purpose depends.

While older institutions have benefited from time and history upon which they have built a concrete, well-defined center, any institution can use rituals to construct, reinforce, and communicate its center. Centeredness requires that ritual participants regularly incorporate the founding beliefs into the structure and practice of the ritual. Through the repetition of these beliefs in words, music, and symbols, a strong sense of institutional centeredness can be developed.

Perpetuating the Legacy. In an institution with a firm center, students receive the ritual message that their involvement in the perpetuation of the institution's legacy is essential. Students have an active role in perpetuating the legacy through ritual involvement, conversations about founding beliefs, and honoring the beliefs through their actions and achievements. "Rather than unattached, isolated individuals, the students became part of a whole; part of a community. The belief that disparate points of view can be aligned for at least some period of time can create the momentum for ritual to continue" (Manning, 1989a, p. 229). Their lives are to be conducted in a way that meets or exceeds the lofty expectations of the institution's legacy.

Through their evocative language, ability to draw participants into their action, and capacity to transcend the mundane, rituals meet primordial human needs. Through actions that encourage individuals to feel connected to other people, consider larger issues, and undertake loftier causes, humans are drawn to rituals. Through their uncertainty and creative capacity, rituals appeal to the primordial human need to express sanctity and magic. As such, to continue existing rituals and build new ones is an essential human activity.

CREATING NEW RITUALS

During the student protests and activism of the 1960s and 1970s, the "cute" and "silly" rituals of college life became less meaningful in light of the societal struggles of the time. Students protesting the Vietnam War and political corruption of Watergate grew cynical about campus rituals that seemed to be more fun and games than related to the pivotal events of that era. Disregarding the long-term negative effect to college communities, many rituals and ceremonies were abandoned.

Since the 1960s and 1970s higher education has become more complex and fragmented. As such, colleges and universities need rituals now more than ever before. But, starting new rituals is not a process without controversy or complication. Because these events exist outside the realm of the mind, occupy the feeling dimension of human experience, and touch spiritual and mystical parts of human living, faculty intellectuals and less mature students can underestimate their importance and downplay their effectiveness. Despite this cynicism and skepticism, people need rituals even if they do not think so.

Helpful Features

Some would argue that establishing rituals on today's college campuses is anachronistic. Rituals are something continued from the past. To start a new one in this day and age would appear out of place and irrelevant to students. The approach taken here is that, with significant care, new rituals (a seemingly contradictory term) can be established. But when creating these new rituals, several defining characteristics can be used to better assure success.

A Foundation of Relevant Meaning. The research presented in this book indicates that any new ritual must be consciously built on past practice. Specifically, institutional founding ideas, beliefs, and values must serve as the foundation for the new ritual. Without this reinforcing structure, the new ritual risks misfiring or failing to fire at all. When any ritual fails, the cultural gesture is devoid of meaning. The foundation upon which the tradition rests is weak. Any chance of future success with that particular tradition or others like it will, unfortunately, meet resistance.

Bigger Than Self. If executed skillfully, rituals can be a source of inspiration, insight, and creativity. The action, language, symbols, and other aspects of rituals can and perhaps must engender a connection between community members and ideas larger than themselves. The magic and spirituality of rituals builds the connection between the individual and larger, more significant goals. For the ancients, that "something" was the gods. At Mount Holyoke College, it was nature. At many colleges the "something" is the feeling obtained when connected to or in communion with others. These communal feelings include trust, care, and understanding, all necessary for healthy living.

Reviving Past Rituals. Yearbooks, college archives, and memories of long-term administrators are sources of ideas for rituals to be revived. Because discontinued rituals are often based on founding beliefs and have some record of success, reviving past rituals can result in more success than starting completely new ones. Often old rituals can be revised (words changed, music updated, extra touches inserted) to meet the current needs of the college community.

Recognizing Existing Culture and Traditions. College communities devoid of traditionally identified rituals (convocations, founder's days, baccalaureate) often contain their own unique style of traditions. While students of campus culture readily recognize the rituals generally present at more traditional institutions, a trained eye can also detect newer, less obvious traditions. Architecture, student traffic patterns, and even parking habits create a way of life within a college community that adds to or detracts from the campus ethos.

Making Ceremonial. The success of a new ritual depends on whether the participants can be convinced of its messages. Therefore, they must be conveyed in a way that encourages meaning making. If the messages are too explicit, too easily interpreted, participants are denied the experience of interpreting their own meaning. If the messages are obtuse, too mystical or vague, then participants become confused about the purposes and messages of the ritual.

An effective way to engender meaning-making activities during ritual is through music, language, and symbols. College and university administrators, because of the long history of ritual use in higher education, can utilize a variety of ritual actions and symbols to communicate messages and meaning. Academic regalia, a familiar and readily accessible symbol on college campuses, can be easily utilized. College seals and other symbolic representations are present at nearly every institution. Campus members are most likely familiar with "Pomp and Circumstance" and other ceremonial marches. Music can easily be incorporated into the proceedings.

Unhelpful Features

The following caveats are offered as ritual aspects that are unlikely to guarantee success by those establishing new rituals.

Borrowed Rituals. While many administrators attempt to transplant rituals between colleges (particularly rituals from an alma mater), these adopted versions rarely if ever fit the new environment. The college contexts are rarely similar enough for the ritual, based on a specific set of founding values, to fit the new site. The institution-specific history of past practice upon which the successful ritual was based is completely absent on the new campus.

All institutional settings possess a culture. Every college has an ethos unique to its character. Rituals that may work with tremendous success at a long-established college might fail miserably at a public institution. The region of the country, character of the on- and off-campus students, and predominant activities warrant different approaches to the traditional activities of any campus. Community colleges, recently established institutions, and colleges struggling to redefine obsolete beliefs can mistakenly build traditions on a foundation foreign to their existing ethos. They attempt to embrace a cultural identity that will, most likely, clash with their existing campus culture.

Rather than adopt rituals from other institutions, it is better to create activities that are "ritual-like." A tradition of rituals can be initiated through cultural performances that are not full-blown ceremonies. Picnics, student-run shows, and other traditional events are opportunities to build community and communicate institutional values. Through these less formal cultural performances, community members can gradually become accustomed to experiencing events that mimic the characteristics of rituals. The introduction of formal rituals can build upon this foundation. When over-eager administrators introduce formal rituals on a campus unfamiliar with ritual practice, they risk having the symbols misunderstood, cues concerning ritual behavior missed, and messages miscommunicated.

Devoid of Meaning. Successful rituals are saturated with meaning. As discussed earlier in this book, the multivocal nature of rituals is created, among other mechanisms, through paradox, multifaceted symbols, and abundant opportunities for exegesis. Rituals that lack meaning and opportunities for participants to create meaning cannot help but fail.

Flat and Forced. Finally, rituals must convey emotion. Whether joyful, raucous, or solemn, rituals cannot be flat. The vivid memories created through ritual are linked to the feelings created during their enactment. While it is a fine balance between forcing the emotions and simply letting them flow unabated, rituals must be stimulating, moving, and passionate.

Resistance to Rituals

Despite the fact that people, especially students, participate in rituals they do not fully believe (Grimes, 1990), rituals' influence should not be underestimated. Ambivalence about rituals often means that challenge, complexity, and uncertainty are present. The complexity created through resistance and ambivalence is often the most interesting part of the ritual. The dynamism created through this circumstance of partial belief-partial disbelief creates a situation where truths are questioned, beliefs are open to revision, and behaviors are changed.

In addition to feeling resistance and ambivalence, participants can perform the actions of rituals without believing the messages communicated. This circumstance is evident to anyone who has wandered away from the religious tradition in which he or she was raised and then attends a service as an adult. One can know, recite, and even recall verbatim, the words, invocations, and prayers of the service. Yet, the truth of these words no longer rings true for the hearer.

But the magic of ritual action warrants that one exhibit care as he or she speaks words that may not be true. The form of ritual and the power of the context in which the words are spoken can create a circumstance where the beliefs catch you off guard. As a respondent from this research expressed, you find yourself believing before you know it.

The research in this book confirms that students, while vocally skeptical concerning rituals, often withhold final judgment about their value. This suspension of belief is evident when students call the rituals "silly" but attend them all the same.

CONCLUSION

In summary, starting new rituals can be fraught with pitfalls, false starts, and great joy. If one remembers as well as takes advantage of the created reality of rituals and culture, successful "new" traditions are possible. Humans can do anything within the bounds of culture because it is their creation.

Chapter 14

Alumnae Parade and Laurel Chain

"When you are a freshman you think that all these traditions are pretty silly, but let
me tell you I can't wait to carry my leaves!"
                                    —Senior respondent and Black student
                                    leader several weeks before graduation

Few students in the dormitories discussed the option of *not* attending the events of
Alumnae Weekend and graduation. By the senior year, after three years of exposure
to rituals, persuasion to their messages, and tug of peers toward community
activities, students were pulled into the rituals. Conversations over dinner entailed
recent purchases of white dresses and white shoes as well as the specific logistics of
the upcoming events. Were the white dresses worn for baccalaureate,
commencement, or only for the Laurel Chain? Confusion reigned over the imprecise
descriptions passed on by word of mouth.

On the morning of the Laurel Chain and Alumnae Parade the clock tower bell
sounded its usual half-hour call and then continued to peal. It was time to line up by
class for the Parade.

THE ALUMNAE PARADE

Gathering in Advance

Alumnae, arranging themselves by class and color, gathered around the college
green in advance of the Parade. Excitement built as they lined up, greeted old
friends, and welcomed new ones. Alumnae from the classes of '08, '23, '38, '63, and
'86 were the alumnae participants for this year's Reunion Weekends. The senior
class, scheduled to bring up the rear of the Parade, seemed young in contrast to the
classes celebrating their eightieth, fiftieth, twenty-fifth, and second reunions. All
were dressed in white dresses and white shoes, the traditional garb for the Parade
and Laurel Chain. One had to wear white or else break the tradition.

Despite the fact that graduation was held during Reunion Weekend, that
culminating ritual was not the reason that alumnae returned to the college. They
returned to demonstrate their devotion to the college community. The Alumnae
Parade upstaged graduation, the milestone of a college career. The Parade, yearly

alumnae association meetings, and events centered in the dormitories excluded seniors. In fact, undergraduates believed that the emphasis on alumnae took away from the graduation ceremonies as students were asked to double up in the dormitories to make room for visiting alumnae.

Any negative feelings the students had about their struggles with the academic rigor, loneliness of the limited social life, and doubts whether they could get through the intense intellectual challenge were temporarily set aside. The negative aspects of the academic challenge and difficult personal times at the college faded as alumnae gathered with old friends, made new ones, and continued to build a fierce devotion to the community and college. According to a nonalumna admissions administrator, the alumnae "drop everything when Mount Holyoke calls." While discussing alumnae, an alumnae office administrator who was also an alumna said, "Ceremonies create an opportunity to show that devotion."

Placards, Class Colors, and Costumes

Respondents commented that the Alumnae Parade was great entertainment. Alumnae collaborate by class to devise costumes and sayings for the placards lettered by the alumnae office. The placards made statements and recalled events of that class experience.

Hardware meant hardware. Software wasn't a word.

We're more "traditional" than we'd ever have dreamed!

The first 80th reunion ever!

Two dorms ablaze made the front page.

Octogenarians we may be but while we're on campus we're just 23!!

Yellow balloons floating in the sky made these sophomores really cry!!

Mount Holyoke prepared us for almost anything . . . And we've seen almost everything!!

We're more assertive now—And don't you forget it!!

We celebrate 150 years of remarkable women!!

These sayings presented a real sense of history.

Walking canes, hats, umbrellas, and T-shirts coordinated by class color made up the costumes. Four colors and symbols cycled through the classes: red and Pegasus, green and griffin, yellow and sphinx, and blue and lion. Balloons, streamers on cars, and the lettering of the placards announced both the color of the class and the events that made up their history. The symbols of the individual classes were incorporated into the signs, costumes, and parade paraphernalia. The colors and symbols stayed with a class from freshman year through reunions as alumnae.

As alumnae gathered by class, one saw the changes that had taken place over the years. Faces became progressively younger as the line stretched toward the graduating class gathered at the Parade's rear. All the alumnae reflecting Mount Holyoke's emphasis on an active, fit lifestyle, appeared surprisingly young. The alumnae who came to the reunion weekend were clearly leading active lives.

Top hats proudly displaying "'63" were worn by the twenty-fifth reunion class. Walking canes finished the costumes that served to accent their white outfits. The fiftieth reunion class, '38, had academic hoods of blue and red. The alumnae looked regal in a scholarly way as they gathered under the trees. Another reunion class, '86, celebrated their reunion with class-red fire hats. They were graduating seniors when a local inn burned through arson and touched off a drive to rejuvenate South Hadley's village center. Only six members of the Class of '23 were present but their yellow Hawaiian leis declared their class color.

The Laurel

The newest group to experience the pageant that transformed students into alumnae was gathering at the end of the line. Excitement grew as an alumna administrator and former director of observances rolled out the laurel chain. The chain was carried by the senior class as part of the Parade and eventually draped over the wrought iron fence of the founder's grave. In the early days of the Alumnae Parade and Laurel Chain, seniors cut the laurel from surrounding woods and fashioned it into the chain. But those ceremonial treks into the nearby woods to cut and collect the laurel were no longer part of the tradition. According to state laws, wild laurel could no longer be picked. The laurel was now grown, cut, and fashioned into the long chain by a local florist. The cost had been assumed by the senior class until the 1970s when sparse class finances and a changing political climate on campus precipitated a class decision to eliminate the expensive chain. The college now assumed the cost of the laurel chain rather than see the tradition abandoned.

Buying rather than picking the laurel was not the only change in the ritual during the 1970s. Several respondents identified that era as one of change in the college in general and specifically in the Laurel Chain ritual. The white dresses, gathering of alumnae, and unity symbolized by the chain made the Alumnae Parade and Laurel Chain the most sentimental of traditions. The students of the 1970s, rebellious in the face of an unpopular war, the freedoms of the sexual revolution, and upheaval on college campuses, disapproved of the tradition. Although fiercely loyal to the college, they were uninterested in roots and traditions. One respondent described the students of that time as belligerent; these students had very negative opinions about the college and American society in general. Alumnae respondents who attended Mount Holyoke during those tumultuous times reported that the Class of 1971 did not carry laurel but donated the money to an anti-Vietnam War cause. They participated in the Alumnae Parade in blue jeans rather than the white dresses. Although many continued to support the decision made during the "best" and "most exciting" time to go to college, in retrospect, others conveyed to the secretary of the college that they were "sorry, now that we didn't carry the laurel chain and sing Bread and Roses." An alumna dormitory head resident and former class president commented, "Tradition was really important as a senior. It serves as a real anchor to the place."

Despite individual class perspectives, the traditions survived that difficult chapter in American higher education. At Mount Holyoke, creative ways were found to finance and perpetuate rituals such as the Alumnae Parade and Laurel Chain. Students who were more sentimental about the past reinstated rituals and traditions discontinued by previous classes. As tempers calmed and sentiment eased over the years, white was worn during the Alumnae Parade once again. The white dresses made the event lovely—"thrilling" even, as a Class of '21 alumna respondent described it. A senior respondent concurred as she described the graduation weekend events. "Last year was the first time I stayed for graduation. The laurel ceremony was so beautiful—better than graduation."

The Parade Route

Each year the route for the Parade wound through the college green, past the steps upon which the platform party stood, and made its way to Mary Lyon's grave. The platform party included Mount Holyoke's president, the alumnae association president, and newly elected junior and senior class presidents. All were, of course, dressed in white. An alumnae administrator reported that the president was "one person who seems to try and incorporate the rituals and traditions into her job as president. She does not trivialize them. This seems important for their continuation." Continuity was important to the practice of these rituals. Several respondents reported that the building steps upon which the review party stood had been the site of Step Sings and class competitions abandoned in the 1940s.

Students, administrators, parents, faculty, family, and friends lined the parade route waiting for the festivities to begin. An alumna, Class of '63 administrator respondent, reminisced that there was "nothing as tear jerking" as the annual Alumnae Parade and grave ritual. Anyone was apt to cry. A younger, Class of '84 respondent agreed: it "sounds corny," but the parade is "so moving." Participating in it is fun but being on the sidelines, watching the long line of alumnae, and reading the signs is even more interesting.

The "Long White Line"

The sounds of the Connecticut Foot Guard Band, originally dispatched by that state's governor, an alumna of Mount Holyoke, signaled that the Parade was beginning. Marching at the front of the long line of white-clad women, the band stopped to pay respects to the reviewers before turning into the green. Their music accompanied the marchers as they passed by the audience and reviewers. The band stood out not just because they were men among all the women but because their Revolutionary garb is such a part of New England history.

The first and oldest class appeared shortly after the Foot Guard. This year, three members of the class of 1908 participated in the Parade. These women, each at least one hundred years old, allowed the college to boast that this was the first eightieth reunion when more than one class member was able to attend. Dressed in white with class color blue ribbons in their hair they rode in antique automobiles. The charm of the old cars concealed the fact that the older alumnae could no longer walk the parade route. The president and her husband moved off the steps to greet the class of 1908 when their cars stopped before the reviewing stand. Blue balloons decorated the cars and flew alongside as they drove by.

The kindness and attention showered on these older alumnae was striking. Students were employed to take care of their every need during the older women's stay on campus. These women were interviewed by local television stations, lauded in speeches, and entertained at dinners in their honor. Although a student joked about being on the "wheelchair brigade," it was evident in the way that she spoke of these women's accomplishments that she admired the stamina and tenacity of these centenarians. Through the actions toward these oldest alumnae, college members revealed their fierce devotion. The role of the older alumnae as symbols of the strength and tenacity of Mount Holyoke was recognized.

The class year of each group was proudly announced by a banner sporting year and class color. The banners, purchased when the classes were students, were resurrected for reunions. Placards were held high as the Parade proceeded. The standard alumnae office lettered signs were accompanied by less artistic homemade versions.

We support a diverse college.

We support the lesbian alumnae network.

These unofficial placards revealed that not all were uniformly welcomed in this community.

A Class of '84 alumna respondent thought the messages written on the placards, including the unofficial ones, and the long white line of the Alumnae Parade showed the "kind of strength that this body of women embodies." The strength existed because the signs were so truthful. In her opinion people just are not that truthful in other circumstances. But with these women, there was something about the support of one another that led them to be truthful about themselves.

The class of 1938, looking vital and energetic, marched in the Parade for their fiftieth reunion. They graduated prior to World War II and saw tremendous changes in the college: campus buildings razed and re-built, new careers introduced, course offerings expanded, and student diversity increased. As the Parade rolled by, the faces got progressively younger.

The long parade of alumnae was a visible symbol of the support nurtured in these women as students. The director of observances, an administrator in charge of Fall Convocation, Founder's Day, Baccalaureate, and Commencement, linked support and the college's rituals. "This is where the bigger rituals come into play . . . the support system becomes visible . . . The long white line . . . It's incredible. It's very moving." One could just see the support as they were marching. "Support is also evident amongst classes that aren't 're-unioning.' Many classes have set up a person-to-person network to aid classmates who are experiencing trauma—divorce, death of a child or spouse, caring for aging parents, loss of a job, etc. People in need have hooked up with others who have experienced the same sort of thing," commented an alumna administrator. There was a feeling that there were networks that were "very real." And you "feel them all the time."

Relationships and connectedness were made most visible during the Alumnae Parade and Laurel Chain but this feeling of closeness and support was present every day. The secretary of the college, a non-alumna administrator, described the feeling that people "love Mount Holyoke—and they share that love." Standing and watching the Parade one could feel the generations of daughters of the college.

Feelings arose from the communion so visibly expressed, the alumnae's costumes and dress of the students, the long white line of support, and the stamina of the women who returned for Reunion. Alumnae and students admitted that this ritual may be the only time they feel such support, communion, and sense of self. Respondents commented that rituals and traditions exist in colleges that have a strong sense of self and the ability to engender self-esteem among their participants.

The Laurel Chain

Applause and excitement grew as the seniors, smiling, visibly happy and enthusiastic, appeared with the Laurel Chain and marched up the knoll to the founder's grave. Similar to the alumnae they followed, the majority of the class chose to participate in the ritual.

Mary Lyon's grave was both a symbol of the important truths of the college and of its myths. As a final resting place of the founder, the grave represented her founding ideals. The stature of these ideals was matched by the prominence of the grave, which was placed high on a hill surrounded by carefully tended lawns, trees, and paths. Since it was located in the center of campus, students could not avoid walking past it on their way to class, laboratories, the library, and dormitories. The truths and ideals central to the college's mission were reinforced by the founder's epitaph indelibly etched on her headstone: "There is nothing in the universe that I fear, but that I shall not know all my duty or fail to do it."

The grave supported the mythical stories of Mary Lyon as controversy raged over her true burial place. Was she buried in the campus mound, exhumed, and buried elsewhere? In total, three locations claimed to be the final resting place of her remains.

Marching alumnae, arriving at the grave site, stopped and lined the road in a double row. Seniors, as rising alumnae, passed through the gauntlet of cheering, applauding alumnae. Senior respondents talked about the emotion evoked by walking through the generations of alumnae. These women knew firsthand what it meant to be a Mount Holyoke student. Their support and enthusiasm meant the world to this graduating class. The words of a religion professor spoken during a Baccalaureate speech the previous day previewed the effect of the gauntlet of alumnae: "Those who came before you have cut a wide path." The past, present, and future came together during the ritual in the form of alumnae and seniors. The traditions and feelings were passed from oldest to youngest alumnae.

The line of seniors, waving to those gathered on the roadside, marched through the towering trees up the rise to the founder's grave. Each was surrounded by her friends and classmates. Any contrived order of the alphabet was abandoned. The supportive relationships were what was important, and seniors grouped together by friendships and dormitory groups. Everyone—alumnae, parents, and visitors—stood in the grass and pushed against the thin yellow twine that cordoned off the grave area.

Continuous clapping sounded as an outpouring of support and understanding rose from the alumnae. One could feel how proud the alumnae participants were of these women who made the choice to take a more difficult route: single-sex college, academic rigor, and personal challenge. The parents were proud, too, but the alumnae better understood the challenges faced and met for they, too, had experienced the struggle. The seniors wound around the grove and traversed the gravel path to the grave. The older classes seated in chairs in the grove rose to their feet as the seniors walked through the generations of alumnae.

The rehearsals for the ritual had done the trick. Although not quite sure where they would end up, for the sake of the ritual as described by the dean of the college chapel, they were "willing to be led" by the class officers. Only minor confusion reigned as seniors wove around one another. Though not particularly neat, the laurel chain ended up on the outside of the cluster of women.

The president of the college and alumnae president joined the graduating class at the gate of the grave. A ripple of excitement and a cheer went through the seniors as the Laurel Chain was passed overhead and draped over the fence. The pageantry and fun of it all was "amazing."

"Bread and Roses," a song sung by the women textile workers in the mills of Massachusetts in the 1800s, was traditionally sung by seniors and alumnae. Controversy raged among the students that the practice of singing the feminist song, started by seniors during a more radical time than the present, had little meaning for them. Few knew the words, origins, or significance of the song. But the feeling persisted that the song embodied the college's spirit and, therefore, should be continued. Sung for more than ten years, it had become a tradition. The flyers containing the words to "Bread and Roses" fell to the ground as the more familiar Alma Mater was begun. Faculty, administrators, alumnae, and parents joined in the singing.

The seniors were at the end of a process begun with the welcoming ritual of Convocation. During that time and throughout the process they shared a significant amount with the college and gained a great deal in return. Commencement, which occurred on the day following the Alumnae Parade and Laurel Chain, ushered them into the outside world. But on the day of the Parade, they felt and knew, as voiced by a senior respondent, that "this is my home."

A Most Private Ritual

The ritual at the grave was private and intended for the seniors. For those who had not graduated from the college, their role was one of spectator. The feeling of commonality and unity among the alumnae and seniors was not one that many in the audience would experience or understand. A continuity of experience and feeling was passed from past to present student. A senior respondent described this continuity between alumnae and students: "When you see all these alumnae, you know that you are spanning time—that you are part of history. You are part of a non-stopping, never-ending tradition." The students were thrilled to be part of the history, to be one of the dauntless women who attended the college and shared the accomplishments produced.

The Laurel Chain and Alumnae Parade lauds the women of Mount Holyoke who provide each other support, challenge, and celebration. In alumnae and rising alumnae alike, there was an evident joyousness, an understanding about what had been accomplished, and what would be achieved in the future. This understanding was accompanied by deep emotion. Respondents reported that it was not unusual to see people weeping openly during the Laurel Chain. This is an event that inspires such emotions.

The impact of the students' actions during the Alumnae Parade and Laurel Chain may not be realized until years after graduation. After they graduate, students often come to understand what they experienced. Those experiences take on increased significance in retrospect. An alumna administrator and assistant to the president described her ambivalent feelings: "I didn't come back . . . until my twentieth reunion. I was very cynical when I left as a senior. You start talking to other alumnae and you realize the richer fabric of the rituals which you have in common." The Laurel Chain and Alumnae Parade could become an opportunity for these women to come back and grow into a renewed awareness. In the moment of the ritual's creation, experience, feelings, and commonality are perpetuated and passed on.

In light of the challenges and pride of attending Mount Holyoke, the graduating seniors and alumnae share a strong bond of sisterhood. This bond and connection to the college's values were linked by an alumna administrator to the rituals and traditions: "The traditions are the only constant. It was something that people can count on. The whole place could be going to hell but the traditions will go on. There will be that Laurel Chain." The enactment of this ritual was a practice of commitment, constancy, and continuity.

Ritual-Inspired Emotions

A multitude of feelings existed during the Laurel Chain and Alumnae Parade. A prominent emotion involved keeping the spirit of the college alive. Both alumnae and students acknowledged they have been through something special and unique from other college experiences. An alumna respondent struggled to describe the experience: "It is difficult to explain to someone who has not gone to the college the significance of the Laurel Chain . . . But it creates a common bond among the people who have attended the college." The director of observances commented that the purpose of ritual is to "bind the community together." The strength of the feeling toward the community is symbolized by the extent to which the rituals survive. She said, we "talk a lot here about a sense of community—and you have to demonstrate that." We "need *more* rituals to pull the College together."

LAUREL CHAIN AND ALUMNAE PARADE INTERPRETATIONS

The participants, through their actions in the Alumnae Parade and Laurel Chain, honored the founder, expressed class and college pride, and celebrated the close relationships formed among students. The Laurel Chain is a tribute to the seniors within the context of honoring the founder. The tribute is expressed through a tradition established long before the seniors chose the college as their alma mater. The Parade brought them to the graceful setting of the grove to celebrate their being together as well as their accomplishments as women of scholarship. Mary Lyon and the ideals she inspired in the college members were honored in nearly every action during the Alumnae Parade and Laurel Chain. Her ideals of achievement, leadership, and community spoke through every action of the ritual. The climax of the event, held at her grave, symbolized the central place she continued to occupy in the college's activities. Participants honored each other as women marched in chronological order by graduating class (oldest classes in the honored positions at the head of the Parade). This connecting bond, expressed as a similarity of experience through generations of alumnae, was made visible by a similarity of dress and action. Class pride was symbolized by banners, accessories in class color, and lettered signs documenting their experiences as a class.

The emotions that characterized these events were built through the powerful image of support embodied in the long white line as well as the generational crescendo culminating with the senior class. The bonding of alumnae and seniors was dramatically illustrated through the chain of laurel that symbolized unity. With the chain linking them, seniors marched together as one body.

Uniquely Female Relationships

The generational order of classes was seen by some respondents as representing the relationships among the women. Mother/daughter relationships existed among and within the older and younger alumnae. Sister relationships existed among and within classes. An inheritance was given by the fiftieth reunion class of 1938 to their daughters in the class of 1988. The money was designated as an endowment to be used for '88s fiftieth reunion. Siblinglike relationships were evident during the post-parade alumnae meeting as classes sang "sister songs" and addressed aspects of the sisterhood to which they belonged (i.e., achievements of classmates, common experiences between classes spanning fifty or more years). The public ritual and symbols of the Parade (laurel, white dresses, and Parade order) symbolized unity, community, and devotion. The Parade embodies the ideal of women's community as it extends over time. This community is visually expressed in the Alumnae Parade, the unbroken line of alumnae—oldest to youngest.

Communitas

Victor Turner (1969) discussed an emotional, uniting phenomenon he termed communitas. Turner described communitas as spontaneous, immediate, elusive, seamless, and structureless. During moments of communitas, structure is less evident as emotions reign. Groups of people act as one when emotion ripples through the crowd and coordinated action transpires without words or instruction.

A moment of communitas occurred during the Laurel Chain. Close unity was conveyed as identically dressed women grouped tightly around the grave, making it difficult to separate one face from another. The emotional closeness so often discussed by respondents was reinforced with physical closeness. During the Alumnae Parade and Laurel Chain, individual differences among the women (age, experience, race, class) blended for at least the brief instant of communitas. Participants dressed alike, synchronized their movements, and jointly recited or sang a prewritten script and score. In the name of community, their commonality of beliefs, or simply the desire to be part of the action, the seniors created a sense of oneness through their actions during the Alumnae Parade and Laurel Chain. Audible cries of celebration from the seniors triggered a ripple of excitement and emotion that passed through the crowd a fraction of a second before the laurel was passed overhead toward the wrought iron fence of the grave. The audience shared in the collectivity experienced by the seniors and alumnae by visually experiencing the communitas and emotionally feeling their celebration. The visual effect of the white dresses, the symbolism of the seniors' passage through a double row of cheering alumnae, and the feeling of collectivity created as the laurel chain corralled the seniors into a unified group built the emotional peak necessary for the spontaneous, instantaneous communitas.

SUMMARY

Rituals as powerful as the Laurel Chain and Alumnae Parade are rare occurrences. The intensification of the feelings of the group and common bond built through their actions occur only on special occasions. If these rituals happened every day, their commonplace nature would inhibit them in forming bonds, passing feelings to subsequent classes, and building traditions. Rituals this powerful also do not occur spontaneously. Four years of sharing beliefs, values, and individual and communal histories for the individual and one hundred fifty years of legacy for the institution culminate in these annual events.

Chapter 15

Constructivist Inquiry and Higher Education Rituals

> The search for a consistent explanation of human social behavior through a model
> of rational intent and an imputation of intent from action has had some successes.
> But there is no sign that the university is one of the successes, or very likely to
> become one (Cohen & March, 1986, p. 196).

Research in education has a long history of quantitative methods, causal attributions,
and search for logical and rational motives underlying the actions of participants
(Lucas, 1985; Wolcott, 1984). Conventional methods based on rationality to explain
complexity have created an illusion of order and harmony in human interaction. But
despite success with quantitative methods in some areas, they fall short of explaining
the complexities and paradoxes of colleges and universities.

The data for the study reported in this book was collected and analyzed using
a qualitative approach called constructivist inquiry. This method has been labeled
postpositivistic, ethnographic, phenomenological, subjective, case study approach,
hermeneutic, and humanistic (Guba & Lincoln, 1989; Lincoln & Guba, 1985). With
its roots in ethnography and phenomenology (Guba, 1978; Skrtic, 1985),
constructivist inquiry is "a pattern or model for how inquiry may be conducted"
(Guba & Lincoln, 1982, p. 233). At the root of the assumptions underlying
constructivist inquiry is the emergent, nonconventional paradigm that acknowledges
the complexity, contradiction, and paradox inherent to social living.

The techniques of constructivist inquiry (interviews, document analysis, and
observation) require face-to-face contact with the respondents as well as the
presence of the researcher at the research site. Document analysis can supplement
findings discovered through interviews and observations. But discovery through
constructivist inquiry entails talking with people, discovering what is important to
them, and working with them to jointly construct interpretations of the events based
on their ideas about those events. Throughout these studies, human action was the
focus of the observation and interviewing. The immediacy of the emotions evoked
and meanings interpreted were primary concerns in the research.

DESIGN OF A CONSTRUCTIVIST INQUIRY

"Few practicing social scientists today believe their research resembles the orderly intellectual presentations in textbooks on method: choice of problem, formulation of hypotheses and testing of them, analysis and interpretation of data" (Powdermaker, 1966, p. 10). A feature of constructivist inquiry is that the design of the study cannot be unequivocally determined in advance. "Rather than a pre-determined structure, the constructivist inquirer begins as an anthropologist might begin learning about a strange culture, by immersing himself [*sic*] in the investigation with as open a mind as possible, and permitting impressions to emerge" (Guba, 1978, p. 13). Openness is the predominant characteristic of the research as the design emerges, changes, and continuously shapes. The design becomes more clear as the researcher becomes familiar with the site, the people who live there, and their practices.

These studies used the anthropological theory of rituals and the methodological assumptions of constructivist inquiry as an informed place from which to begin. These theoretical perspectives provided guidance for the study's focus and boundaries. The theory was not used to formulate the interview questions, construct a priori decisions in classifying events, or build preconceived categories for data analysis. I familiarized myself with the college, participants, and practices by reading student handbooks, orientation literature, publications, and information forwarded to me by gatekeepers.

ASSUMPTIONS OF THE UNDERLYING PARADIGM

The positivist paradigm that has dominated educational research relies on scientific inquiry or empiricism as its inquiry mode. The paradigm assumptions include (a) an objective reality relying on the subject/object dichotomy, (b) a uniform nature extending through space and time, and (c) effects that can be traced and related to causes (Guba & Lincoln, 1989; Lincoln & Guba, 1985). In conventional research tradition, the world is intelligible and directly accessible to investigation. Phenomena that cannot be measured do not exist. Measurement is primarily conducted using paper and pencil instruments whose data are converted to numbers susceptible to statistical analysis. This empirical measure of human action and the resulting "unbiased" conclusions are "accurate" only in so much as they use a detached and objective observer (Guba & Lincoln, 1989; Lincoln & Guba, 1985; Lucas, 1985).

CONSTRUCTIVIST INQUIRY AXIOMS

Constructivist inquiry is underscored with axioms that are congruent with the interpretive nature of the studies reported in this book (Guba, 1985; Guba & Lincoln, 1982, 1989; Lincoln & Guba, 1985; Smircich, 1986; Smith, 1990).

Axiom Number One: Reality

Realities are multiple, constructed, and holistic (relativist ontology) (Guba & Lincoln, 1982, 1986, 1989; Lincoln & Guba, 1985; Smith, 1983, 1990). The meanings derived from participation in the rituals will be multiple and socially constructed by the participants. The mutually shaping action of the community's people, including the participants and respondents, and multiple realities acknowledged by the constructivist paradigm differ sharply with the subject/object dualism of the conventional paradigm.

By contrast the conventional paradigm assumes that a sharp distinction can be drawn between the action of the respondents and those of the researcher. Research can be conducted in such a way that the inquirer does not affect the participants' action. According to this perspective, the inquirer can observe the activities being researched from a distant, unobtrusive viewpoint. This objectivity is possible because of the existence of a singular objective reality, unchanged by the idiosyncratic nature of the respondents and researcher.

The constructivist paradigm, on the other hand, assumes that there are multiple realities intimately related to the perceptions, beliefs, individual histories, and characteristics of respondents, participants, and the researcher. Any "inquiry into these multiple realities will inevitably diverge (each inquiry raises more questions than it answers) so that prediction and control are unlikely outcomes although some level of understanding (*verstehen*) can be achieved" (Lincoln & Guba, 1985, p. 37). The understandings and meanings derived from research based on the constructivist paradigm are part of the whole, understood only as viewed in the context in which the meanings expressed. For example, ritual interpretation must consider college cultural aspects that influence, shape, and serve to define the participants' complex social practices.

Constructed and multiple realities, in the constructivist perspective, are chaotic or, at the very least, inconsistent. Constructivist researchers assume that understanding social reality will be difficult. Individual human beliefs make reality complex and elaborate. Idiosyncratic beliefs lead to multiple realities; any reductionist or singular view of reality is simplistic and provides a weak explanation.

Constructivist researchers make sense of and understand participants' multiple realities by examining the research setting holistically. They use metaphors to explain complexity by relating the understanding of the context's part to the culture's whole. The metaphoric explanation attempts to retain complexity and lend understanding.

For example, the Mount Holyoke respondents offered metaphors (cyclical, revolutionary, generational, and evolutionary) to explain, describe, and interpret the rituals (Manning, 1994a). As the research progressed, these metaphors were incorporated into the questions asked of respondents. This yielded additional metaphors as well as further understanding of the individuals' meanings and the interpretations formulated by them.

Axiom Number Two: Researcher and Researched Relationship

In the constructivist paradigm, researchers and respondents are interactive and inseparable (monistic, subjectivist epistemology) (Guba & Lincoln, 1982, 1989; Lincoln & Guba, 1985; Smith, 1983, 1990). A goal of qualitative research is to minimize the distance between the researcher and respondents (Van Maanen, 1979). This goal acknowledges that the researcher and respondent are intrinsically related in such a way that respondents are affected by the actions of the researcher and vice versa (Guba & Lincoln, 1986, 1989; Smith, 1983, 1990). The researcher's presence, as part of the context in which the study occurs, influences the people and actions observed (Capra, 1984). The findings are a creation of the inquiry process rather than a reality that exists in the researcher's absence.

Axiom Number Three: Product of the Inquiry

In constructivist inquiry, time- and context-bound working hypotheses are the research goals (hermeneutic methodology) (Ely, 1991; Erlandson, Harris, Skipper, & Allen, 1993; Guba & Lincoln, 1982, 1986, 1989; Lincoln & Guba, 1985; Smith, 1983, 1990). Time, history, dynamism, and change are essential aspects of any study. Practice and the interpretations about that practice grow from individual and communal experiences rooted in history and recreated in the present (Giddens, 1979, 1984). Idiographic working hypotheses grounded in time and context (rather than nomenthetic generalizations and predictions meant to transcend context, time, and history) are the basis of research interpretations.

An assumption underlying the constructivist inquiry reviewed in this book is that the generalizations and long-term predictions of conventional paradigm studies can only be applied to stable, isolated, recurrent systems (Popper, 1959). Generalizations about rituals cannot be transported to another context without distortion of the understandings about the college under study or distortion of the characteristics of the receiving context. The "same" rituals in a different setting have a different meaning unique to that college's history, context, and distinctiveness.

In contrast to the stability required for research generalizations, human communities are constantly changing. Constructivist inquiry partially reconciles the dynamism of human communities by stating the research findings as working hypotheses rather than generalizations. Working hypotheses are interpretations that reflect and/or explain the data generated from the research (Lincoln & Guba, 1985).

The interpretations resulting from the ritual research and described in the case studies within this book are, at best, a snapshot of a single period of time. The snapshot is a flat representation, capturing only what is accessible to the camera's lens when the shutter is released. The history of the participants, characteristics present but obstructed, and depth of the setting alluded to but not explicit are missed. Furthermore, even if the lens could capture all there was to see, the photo could never fully explain. The dynamic, ever changing nature of human action changes before the picture is formed, shutter closed, and the image registered on film. Despite this expansive and dynamic nature of human action, the study *can* add to understanding within the boundaries of the context with its confines of time and history.

Research findings are a result of negotiated and joint understandings of the respondents and the researcher (Guba & Lincoln, 1986; Smith, 1983). This negotiation and mutual understanding result from analysis, critique, reiteration, and further analysis. Through a hermeneutic process (Lincoln & Guba, 1986) data are integrated with prior observations, built upon, incorporated into the working hypotheses, and changed in light of ongoing data collection. Data are factual but constructed.

For example, in the Mount Holyoke study, ideas about and interpretations of ritual meaning were expressed by respondents during interviews. The ideas were used in subsequent interviews with the same and different respondents to construct working hypotheses. These interpretations were then changed, expounded upon, discarded, and/or left unchanged as further data from interviews and observations were collected, analyzed, and built into working hypotheses and interpretations.

Axiom Number Four: Causality

The constructivist paradigm assumes that entities are in a state of mutual simultaneous shaping, so that it is impossible to distinguish causes from effects (Guba & Lincoln, 1982, 1986, 1989; Lincoln & Guba, 1985; Smith, 1983, 1990). In keeping with this assumption, the dialectical relationship between the social structure and the participants' actions or practices became a theoretical assumption of these studies. Structure and practice form each other in a dynamic and processual interplay (Giddens, 1979). Neither the social structure nor the participants' practice are the sole determinants of the other but are mutually shaping.

Many rituals in this study had a hierarchical structure (authority emanating from the top), subordinate (deferent) and superior (more powerful) participant roles, and spatial arrangements and staging (those higher in the bureaucracy prominently featured in an elevated position). The hierarchical structure of a ritual was created and re-created through the action of participants as they agreed to be led, marched, and followed those in charge. Simultaneously, the participants' action was modeled upon the structural template formed through past practice. An understanding of rituals and their meanings emerged through a comprehension of the relationships among practice, social structure, human action, history, and context.

Axiom Number Five: Role of Values

The constructivist paradigm assumed that all inquiry is value bound (Guba & Lincoln, 1982, 1986, 1989; Lincoln & Guba, 1985). Value judgments and commitments cannot be avoided in the research process. "Value," in this context, means the ideologies of the setting, researcher, respondents, research method, and guiding theory. These influences, which form the culture of the situation, are extremely complex and time dependent. Values "impinge on inquiry and could not meaningfully be excluded, even if it were possible epistemologically to do so" (Skrtic, 1985, p. 214). The researcher brings aspects of him or herself to the study, thereby influencing the research (Griffin, 1986).

The researcher arrives at the site with cultural baggage. This "baggage" influences what one looks for and sees during the research. A researcher with egalitarian values would interpret rituals in a different manner than a researcher with conservative values. Both the researcher and respondents use their individual differences as a way to view their world.

A particularly salient feature of the researcher's and respondents' cultural baggage is language. Language influences the perceptions of the rituals and interpretations. The words one uses to describe and explain phenomenon strongly influence the ways one views the inquiry and data. Ritual meaning is expressed by respondents and the researcher through words. For example, this inquiry and the research questions became more informed as I learned the language of the students, faculty, and administrators at the research sites.

Data (e.g., symbols of power, understandings) are strongly influenced by language. They are symbolically and contextually embedded in the culture being studied. Shared histories and time spent together build shared meanings about the data between the researcher and respondents. These shared meanings and mutual interpretations represent multiple points of view, unintended and unanticipated consequences, and variations within the cultural context.

Values to Be Explicated. There are four sets of values to be explicated: the researcher's, the substantive theory, methodological paradigm, and setting (Lincoln & Guba, 1985). Specifically, the values of the researcher could include his or her educational background, treatment of determinism in the underlying theory, ethical guidelines from the methodology, and status relationships among community members. Another researcher with his or her unique background and set of values would produce a different study unique to the setting that he or she encounters and creates. The explication of these values leads the researcher to a fuller and richer understanding of the respondents and their interpretations.

In the Mount Holyoke study, the fact that I am a female with egalitarian and liberal values congruent with the college's mission played a significant role in the positive reception and cooperation I received. My strong and obvious feminist point of view enabled me to build trust and gain confidence among respondents. My requests for interviews and observations were accommodated on all occasions. I was treated with the utmost care and consideration. Respondents often made comments alluding to my open-mindedness to their concerns because I am a woman.

DATA COLLECTION

Qualitative researchers make use of interviewing, document analysis, and observation as means for collecting data. So that the reader can understand the means through which the data was collected during these studies, the following topics are explored: purposive sampling, data collection techniques, entry and gatekeeping, and premature closure.

Purposive Sampling

Purposive sampling is a nonrandom method of choosing respondents (Lincoln & Guba, 1985; Patton, 1990). The researcher "*begins* with the assumption that context is critical" (Lincoln & Guba, p. 200) and purposely selects a sample (people to interview, events to observe) providing a rich array of information. The object of purposive sampling is to assure that a multitude of points of view are experienced. It is "intended to maximize the scope and range of information gathered" (Skrtic, 1985, p. 201). Purposive sampling proceeds until the researcher feels that redundant data are collected and the categories formulated are exhausted.

Purposive sampling can occur through the use of the following approaches: (a) selection of extreme or deviant cases (ritual nonparticipants), (b) selection of typical cases (ritual participants), (c) selection of maximum variation (years, class, and experience at the college), (d) selection of critical cases (committee chairs, college president, key administrators, and students), (e) selection of politically important or sensitive cases (students of color, primary gatekeepers), and (f) selection of convenient cases (student acquaintances). The researcher casts "the net for deliberately opposite, deviant, idiosyncratic, and atypical constructions of the world or immediate situation" (Lincoln, 1985, p. 147). Thus the sample is differentiated by a variety of characteristics including political commitment, ethnicity, race, regional origins, religious preference, age, gender, and residence (Geertz, 1973).

Entry and Gatekeeping

In these studies, entry to the rituals and potential respondents were generated by college administrators who served as gatekeepers. The dean of students at Mount Holyoke College was the gatekeeper for that study. The college's archivists, highly involved alumnae, and student leaders were contacted and interviewed as a result of the names generated.

Data Collection Techniques

Data collection in constructivist inquiry involves listening to stories, observing and describing the experiences of the researcher and respondents, interviewing respondents, analyzing archival data, and collecting information from documents (Guba, 1978; Guba & Lincoln, 1982, 1989; Lincoln, 1985; Lincoln & Guba, 1985). The researcher uses "methods that extend understandings . . . looking, seeing, hearing, listening, utilizing non-verbal and tactic cues" (Lincoln, 1985, p. 154). The data collection process is less a matter of looking for repeated entries and explanations than it is of looking for increased understanding about the rituals and college context.

The task of deciding which data to collect is a difficult one as the meaning of the data might be revealed only in hindsight (Eisner, 1981). Because it is impossible to know at the study's onset which activities, respondents, and documents will ultimately be significant, the researcher does not narrow the focus of interview questions with a priori protocols. The "inquiry consists, like a scientific inquiry, in picking out clues . . . with a presumed bearing on the presence of something they appear to indicate" (Polanyi, 1983, p. 31). These clues are traces, glimpses of meaning.

Interviewing. Interviewing is the most useful data collection tool for understanding the past, present, and future through storytelling, questioning, empathic listening, and reconstruction of events. Open-ended questions (Skrtic, 1985) leave the interview in the hands of the respondent to tell his or her story. The researcher suspends judgment, follows curiosity, and/or allows him or herself to be guided by experience and reason.

Interviews in these studies lasted approximately one hour and were based on a set of prepared questions. Despite this preparation, most respondents needed minimal encouragement to begin their recitation about campus rituals. Respondents openly and comfortably shared their ideas about why the events occurred, messages they interpreted through the events, and how other community members viewed the events. Each interview ended with the question, "Is there anyone else you would suggest I talk to?"

The significance of the data is revealed as the data collection proceeds; data are analyzed in the context of other information collected; events and feelings are discussed with respondents; and the research becomes more informed about the context and its culture. Data originally perceived at a glance, through further data analysis and exegesis, become significant clues to understand the subject under study.

Premature Closure

One of the most immediate dangers in qualitative data collection is premature closure—a press to discontinue the data collection because categories are saturated and themes are revealed when in actuality neither process is completed (Skrtic, 1985). Rather data should be "collected until one or more of the following conditions [is] obtained: exhaustion of sources, emergence of saturation in the data (a 'feeling of integration'), and over-extension (excessive dross, a 'feeling of irrelevance')" (Lincoln & Guba, 1985, p. 265).

Careful questions to elicit a respondent's account of the ritual and its meaning coupled with a listening style to hear new and divergent perspectives becomes part of the data collection process. The press toward premature closure may lead one to "hear" only what fits into what one already has concluded. Understanding the experience of another is a skill that takes practice and persistence. Researchers must be wary lest experience lead them to "find what we look for" (Eisner, 1979, p. 173).

Interpretations and joint constructions emerge from conversations with respondents. Categories and integration of those categories into explanatory iterations guide the ongoing data collection and theory construction (Glaser, 1978; Strauss & Corbin, 1990). While this process of data analysis is unfolding, premature closure of the data collection can be avoided by continually making the strange familiar and the familiar strange (Geertz, 1973), remaining open to surprise, being responsive to new insights and willing to see beyond preconceptions about the inquiry.

DATA ANALYSIS

Data analysis in constructivist inquiry is inductive (an open process such that specific data are categorized to form working hypotheses that are context and time dependent) rather than deductive (a closed process such that a priori conclusions are "proven" through the collection of specific bits of data). Inductive analysis resembles a metaphor in the manner that it proceeds from part to whole. Deductive analysis proceeds from whole (null hypothesis) to part (collected data). The goal of analysis is to gain understanding and knowledge of the respondents' remarks and the researcher's observations.

Data analysis is conducted continually and simultaneously with data collection (Glaser & Strauss, 1965, 1967; Skrtic, 1985). Data analysis influences the decisions made about further data collection as well as the organization of existing data.

Constant Comparative Method

In these studies, field notes were duplicated and reduced to heuristically sound bits of information called units (Lincoln & Guba, 1985). A unit could be, among other things, a respondent's comment about a ritual, an observation that contained meaning, or a description of a ritual symbol. These units were printed onto index cards, compared against each other for differences and similarities and sorted into categories. Units were used to build the categories, patterns, and themes for both the description of the rituals and interpretations of the rituals' meanings.

Units are selected with an aim toward understanding. They are compared against one another, placed together by similarities, connections, and conceptual orders. This sorting forces patterns and categories to emerge as well as allowing the meaning of events and respondents' reflections to become clear (Glaser, 1978).

Data Analysis Categories

Categories are context bound, time bound, and problematic. The categories emerging through data analysis have more to do with the ideological beliefs of the respondents and the researcher and the particular characteristics of the community than to any universal "truth" embedded in the data. Another sort of units by the same researcher could result in completely different categories. There is no one absolutely correct sort but only interpretations based on the data collected at a particular time and place. Categories are more fluid, dynamic, and subject to change than is indicated when they appear as permanently written words on an index card.

The particular placement of a unit into a category and the appropriateness of category are determined tacitly (Polanyi, 1983). The researcher must trust that a unit belongs or does not belong in a particular category. This trust emerges from what he or she knows as a result of being immersed in the data and research site. These tacit beliefs are not necessarily spoken but exist as an element that is recognized and felt. For example, the meaning attributed by a respondent to a ritual celebrating academic achievement may feel the same as the meaning attributed to a student-run talent show. The rituals may have little or nothing in common in terms of their enactment and mode of performance, but the meaning conveyed through their scripts and scores may "feel familiar" and encourage the researcher to group units in the same category from two distinctly different rituals.

Grounded Theory

Categories are extended, bridged, collapsed, and integrated in the process of building grounded theory. During the constant comparative process and categorization, theories vie for use in a manner that encourages the researcher to confront, synthesize, and transcend description into the realm of theory (Glaser, 1978).

Multiple iterations of categorization prevent pet theories of the researcher from being seen in the data. Missed categories emerge through subsequent sorting and analysis. The "sorting prevents over-conceptualization and pre-conceptualization, since these excesses fall away as useless when the analyst zeros-in on the most parsimonious set of integrated concepts" (Glaser, 1978, p. 120).

Grounded theory is "patterned; it is open-ended and can be extended indefinitely; and it is discovered empirically rather than expounded a priori" (Lincoln & Guba, 1985, p. 206). Facts are not collected as they "fit" a category derived from theory. The study's grounded theory and interpretations are based on the data rather than vice versa. There are no preconceived categories prior to the discovery of grounded theory.

Grounded theory is more dense, more highly integrated, and wider in scope than a priori theory. Its usefulness depends on the manner in which it is related to the respondents' interpretations, beliefs, and actions. Grounded theory is relevant, modifiable, and transcends the units and categories in a generative manner (Glaser, 1978). This generativity and transcendence moves the grounded theory into the realm of conceptualization and interpretation.

Memo Writing

The formulation of grounded theory is greatly facilitated by memo writing during unitizing and categorization. An analytical memo is a commentary written by the qualitative researcher during field note transcription, unitizing and categorizing, or any other time during the research process. Memos, containing the researcher's insights and emerging theory (Glaser & Strauss, 1965), are sorted with the units "The fruitful paradox of constant memoing is that while they force selection, focus, delimitation and emerging framework, they also continually keep the analyst open to new possibilities of research in related substantive and conceptual areas" (Glaser, 1978, p. 88).

Memoing leads to interpretation by expanding the characteristics and properties of categories, integrating the connections between the categories, generating theory, and drawing relevance between the emerging theories. The process of writing memos and, hence, building grounded theory is fostered by building insights and interpretations during data collection and analysis. (Glaser, 1978). In this sense, the "many-leveled messiness of human social life" (Turner & Turner, 1985, p. 209) can be revealed.

The interpretive nature of constructivist inquiry creates an opportunity to grasp meaning. Without interpretation, the inquiry is simply a description. Interpretation makes linkages between contexts (e.g., individual college to American higher education) and incorporates the complex influences that make up the study. The interpretation, if true to the respondents, leads to understanding and explanation. Through analysis and interpretation, the researcher offers patterns and themes of common beliefs while respecting the individual differences.

Theory is conceptually thin, *only* descriptive and weakly explanatory, if the researcher sorts only units rather than memos (Glaser, 1978). "To skip a step . . . is to produce a theory with less conceptual density, less integration, less conceptual qualification, too much descriptive and conceptual flatness in places, and missed connections" (p. 16). The conclusions expressed in the case studies in this book are descriptive *and* interpretive. Both kinds of explanation are constructed from (a) respondents' interpretations, (b) researcher's attempt to understand the respondents' points of view, (c) values and ideologies forming the researcher's perspective, (d) reflexive understandings (complex understandings built through integrating perspectives), and (e) sensitivity to time and history.

In the analysis that occurred during the case studies writing, I linked individual events to the larger context of higher education. These linkages were not an attempt to generalize or predict from one college to all colleges or vice versa. Rather, the linkages were a recognition of the context's complexity and the influence that national structures have on individual colleges. The colleges studied do not exist in a vacuum but are part of a context where the actions of other colleges affected its community. The activities of one campus were transcended through the exegesis of memoing and linkages to other contexts. The college context was transcended in an attempt to understand complexity.

Working Hypotheses

A working hypothesis is context bound and time dependent as opposed to a generalization that is true in all cases. Working hypotheses do not predict but are dynamic and processual in their attempt to describe and explain social living. The researcher proposes them as explanations with relational connections to the data, and to the ritual and its meaning (Turner, V., 1984). These hypotheses identify common themes, initial interpretations, and consequential reactions. The purpose of inquiry then "is to develop an idiographic body of knowledge; this knowledge is best encapsulated in a series of 'working hypotheses' that describe the individual case; differences are as inherently interesting as (and at times more so than) similarities" (Guba, 1985, p. 85). These working hypotheses are not theories in the sense of truth but models approximating experience (Belenky, Clinchy, Goldberger, & Tarule, 1986). They explain the respondents' interpretations without attributing that perspective to *all* college community members.

In the process of data analysis, categories, understandings, and interpretations are shared with respondents for comment and discussion in an ongoing process of interaction between the researcher and respondents. Respondents are often extremely candid in an ongoing process of interaction between the researcher and respondents. This can result in fine tuning of the interpretations, outright discard of others, and discovery of new ones. Sharing working hypotheses enables the researcher to conduct the study *with* the respondents rather than *to* them.

The word "negotiation" implies an equal sharing of information in the spirit of compromise. My experience with this ritual research indicated that the task of learning the intricacies of someone else's culture is a difficult process. Even in the later stages of data analysis (case study writing and member checks) misconceptions were challenged by respondents. I never understood the rituals to the level experienced by the community's members.

Data analysis continues through the writing of the case studies. Theories are adopted and abandoned, categories focused, and units discarded or sorted into other categories. This analysis is similar to the process of communicating meaning in the rituals. Both processes conveyed the dynamism that exists in vivo. Rather than an abstract structure imposed on the ritual's action, the working hypotheses are a means to understand life and community living.

Interpretation

The working hypotheses and interpretations constructed are limited by the researcher's and respondents' past experience with theories, their ways of making meaning, and the cultural context in which the research took place. Theoretically, endless possibilities of perspectives and theories can be postulated as explanation. But past training, history, and categories of understanding limit themes and patterns (Smith & Hershusius, 1986). For example, training in anthropology and a willingness to consider alternative cultural perspectives gave me a theoretical perspective or lens to use as I collected data, formulated questions for participants, and listened to responses.

Time and history fix the researcher's and respondents' constructions and interpretations in a context. This context is characterized by the ways of being, acting, and believing that compose the sense of place. Themes and patterns conveyed by the respondents reflect the college's history, the values of the community, and its belief systems.

The researcher's interpretation of the respondents' comments approximates but never totally explicates the socially constructed reality of those respondents. "In discussing ritual, an analysis of outcome is always an interpretation and an incomplete one" (Myerhoff, 1984, p. 170). The dynamism and complexity of human living precludes ever *completely* knowing. Interpretation is idiographic in the sense that it is an individual's (the researcher's) interpretation of individuals' (the respondents') interpretation. The inquiry serves its purpose well when these interpretations illuminate rather than demonstrate (Sanday, 1979).

Explanations, never complete, bridge patterns from known to known rather than known to unknown. As such, the interpretations are nontransferable. They cannot be transplanted as indisputable meanings for a college in a different time and place with a different history. Despite this nontransferability there is something to be learned and understood about the community, the beliefs of those people, and the themes agreed upon through practice and history. The purpose is understanding or *verstehen* (Lincoln, 1985; Smith, 1983). *Verstehen* means "to 'live through,' or recreate, the experience of others within oneself" (Smith, p. 7).

In this study, research on rituals can provide insight into the meanings conveyed through these events, the importance of the colleges' missions, the vision of their leaders, and the beliefs of the participants. The research can lend understanding, though not prediction and control, to events at other colleges and universities.

AUTHENTICITY

Constructivist inquiry asserts that there are ways to ensure that the research is conducted in a manner fair to the respondents and reflective of the information they share. Authenticity is a series of processes, concepts, and techniques that facilitate and/or determine the faithfulness of the research (Lather, 1993; Lincoln, 1995; Lincoln & Guba, 1986; Manning, 1997). Authenticity is composed of the concepts of (a) fairness, (b) ontological authenticity, (c) educative authenticity, (d) catalytic authenticity, and (e) tactical authenticity.

Fairness

Fairness addresses whether the researcher has conducted the research in a manner that conveys respect for the respondents and the information they share. Although not explicated in the constructivist inquiry literature, in this study I used the following techniques to ensure fairness: consent forms signed by each respondent, thorough explanation of the study prior to each interview, review of the field notes (including memos and working hypotheses) by the respective respondent, and a review of the draft case study by a group of respondents (grand member check) (Skrtic, 1985).

An issue raised in the Mount Holyoke study relating to fairness was my obtrusiveness as a researcher. My personal preference was to remain in the background of the rituals, but this was not always the best place to observe the rituals. Such behavior also risked creating an ungracious and ungrateful impression on my sponsors. Ethical issues were raised as I became involved in conversations with or overhead dialogue among people who either did not know about my research or thought that our conversations were "off the record." I used my judgment to disregard this information as data but the impressions remained in my thoughts.

Ontological Authenticity

Through the activities of ontological authenticity the consciousness of respondents, participants, and case study readers are raised (Guba & Lincoln, 1989; Lincoln, 1995; Lincoln & Guba, 1986; Manning, 1997). This criteria is met when the dialectical process between the data collection and analysis is made explicit.

The primary activity used to achieve ontological authenticity was an exploratory open-ended manner of conversation between myself and the respondents. This openness created several opportunities for raised consciousness on the part of respondents. Many respondents commented that the interview was the first time that the meaning of the respondents' actions and beliefs about the rituals were spoken aloud. The dialectical discussion between the respondents and myself resulted in a sophisticated and knowledgeable construction of the rituals' meaning.

Educative Authenticity

The third consideration for the criteria of authenticity is educative authenticity (Guba & Lincoln, 1986; Lincoln, 1995; Manning, 1997). Through this criteria, the researcher attempts to build an appreciation for others' constructions in the study's readers. These readers gain a level of understanding of the ritual's meanings as a result of the study's conclusions and interpretations.

Activities to ensure educative authenticity included availability of the case study to the colleges, sharing and soliciting comments about working hypotheses during data analysis, being completely honest about my motivations concerning the research, remaining available for questions, and conveying information when requested.

The primary activity toward educative authenticity was the joint construction of working hypotheses by respondents and researcher. In these studies, respondents were asked to negotiate conclusions and build interpretations about the rituals. Member checking entailed sharing transcribed field notes complete with researcher impressions, commentary, and rudimentary working hypotheses. This activity provided respondents with the opportunity to see their words and ideas from another point of view. The fact that respondents were requested to edit the field notes conveyed an equal partnership where respondents taught the researcher and vice versa. Respondents' comments such as "I never thought of that before," "I don't know—I'm in it now so it's hard," and "I haven't thought all these things out. It's interesting to hear that other people are saying some of the same things" indicated that a learning process was occurring. On many occasions, community members expressed their pleasure that I was conducting research on rituals and stated that the results would be an important account of the college's legacies.

Catalytic Authenticity

Stimulation and facilitation of action is a requirement of catalytic authenticity (Guba & Lincoln, 1985; Lincoln & Guba, 1986; Manning, 1997). The research conclusions and interpretations cannot merely be recorded but should be put to use in a constructive and useful manner.

This study's conclusions could appropriately be used to understand the missions and ideals of higher education institutions in student retention, orientation, and planning. The primary activity to ensure catalytic authenticity was sharing the case studies with those most directly involved in the research.

Tactical Authenticity

The goal of tactical authenticity is empowerment (Lincoln & Guba, 1986). The research, its conclusions, and interpretations should empower the respondents and community members. Tactical authenticity can be achieved by assuring respondent confidentiality; use of consent forms of the study and respondents; choice of interview site by the respondent; open-ended interviewing; and respondent editing of the field notes, memos, and working hypotheses. These processes convey trust and concern for the respondents. An honest account of the uses of their words, ideas, and contributions to the study is essential.

CASE STUDY REPORT

Understandings gained and interpretations constructed through a constructivist inquiry can be reported in a case study format. The case study presents an opportunity for the researcher to perform data analysis toward the goal of understanding. The case study is presented in a novelistic style (quotations from participants, vivid description, researcher as storyteller). The advantages of the case study as a research tool are its ability to build upon the reader's tacit knowledge, demonstrate the interplay between the researcher and respondents, provide thick description, and fix the reader in the setting's context (Lincoln & Guba, 1985). Case studies are often full of contradictory findings and paradoxes (Griffin, 1986) as the researcher/author tries to depict the social setting's complexity. Ultimately, the case study is "describing what is going on and how people are making sense of it" (Wolcott, 1984, p. 184).

The case study is a construction between the author/researcher and the respondents. As such it contains the following elements:

(a) explanation of the problem or research focus,
(b) description of the research setting,
(c) description of the processes relevant to the research focus experienced within that setting,
(d) discussion of the important elements that were studied in depth,
(e) discussion of the outcomes of the research phrased as working hypotheses which add to the understanding of the inquiry (Lincoln & Guba, 1985).

If the case study is written effectively, the reader is caught up in a descriptive, vicarious experience (Lincoln, 1985; Skrtic, 1985). Through the process of data collection, one hears and understands the stories of others. These stories are retold in such a manner that the experience of attending and understanding a ritual is approximated by reading the case study. The researcher in writing the case study and others through case study reading appropriate, absorb, and transform the texts of the respondents (Babcock, 1984). The respondents' feelings and activities of the research setting are vivid.

The case study should convey a sense of the events, people, and experience of the research (Glaser & Strauss, 1965). This familiarity is accomplished by using language common to the college being researched (Smith, 1983). Colloquialisms and common phrases are interspersed in the case; quotations using the respondents' words are quoted; and attempts are made to express local humor.

The case study's form and content interact to increase the effectiveness of the case. That is, the novelistic style and ideas expressed complement each other. The form gives the sense of voice and place experienced during the research (Eisner, 1981); the content is the story.

The case study communicates meaning by remaining open to readers' interpretations. Interpretations and conclusions of the researcher and respondents are transcended and given meaning by the reader.

SUMMARY

This chapter explains the methods and techniques of constructivist inquiry and demonstrates its use in this study of rituals in higher education. The chapter explicates the axioms of constructivist inquiry and attendant new paradigm assumptions. The chapter expands the method in several areas including the concept of authenticity, explanation of context in the study of human action, and interpretive characteristics of working hypotheses.

References

American Council on Education. (1937). *The student personnel point of view*. Washington, D.C.: Author.

American Council on Education. (1949). *The student personnel point of view*. Washington, D.C.: Author.

Ashley, K.M. (1990). *Victor Turner and the construction of cultural criticism: Between literature and anthropology*. Bloomington, IN: Indiana University Press.

Astin, A.W. (1993). *What matters in college? Four critical years revisited*. San Francisco: Jossey-Bass.

Babcock, B. (1984). Arrange me into disorder: Fragments and reflections on ritual clowning. In J. MacAloon (Ed.), *Rite, drama, festival, spectacle: Rehearsals toward a theory of cultural performance* (pp. 102-128). Philadelphia: Institute for the Study of Human Issues.

Babcock, B. (1990). Mud, mirrors, and making up: Liminality and reflexivity in *Between the acts*. In K. Ashley (Ed.), *Victor Turner and the construction of cultural criticism* (pp. 86-116). Bloomington, IN: Indiana University Press.

Bal, M. (1990). Experiencing murder. In K. Ashley, (Ed.). *Victor Turner and the construction of cultural criticism* (pp. 3-20). Bloomington, IN: Indiana University Press.

Baxter Magolda, M.B. (1992). *Knowing and reasoning in college: Gender-related patterns in students' intellectual development*. San Francisco: Jossey-Bass.

Belenky, M., Clinchy, B., Goldberger, N., & Tarule, J. (1986). *Women's ways of knowing: The development of self, voice, and mind*. New York: Basic Books.

Bell, C. (1992). *Ritual theory, ritual practice*. New York: Oxford University Press.

Birnbaum, R. (1991). *How colleges work: The cybernetics of academic organization and leadership*. San Francisco: Jossey-Bass.

Bourdieu, P. (1977). *Outline of a theory of practice*. New York: Cambridge University Press.

Bruner, E.M. (1986). Experience and its expressions. In V.W. Turner & E.M. Bruner (Eds.). *The anthropology of experience* (pp. 3-30). Urbana, IL: University of Illinois Press.

Burns, T., & Laughlin, C. (1979). Ritual and social power. In E.G. d'Aquili, C. Laughlin, & J. McManus (Eds.), *The spectrum of ritual* (pp. 249-279). New York: Columbia University Press.

Capra, F. (1984). *The tao of physics*. New York: Bantam Books.

Chickering, A. (1969). *Education and identity*. San Francisco: Jossey-Bass.

Chickering, A., & Reisser, L. (1993). *Education and identity* (2nd ed.). San Francisco:

Jossey-Bass.

Clark, B. (1972). The organizational saga in higher education. *Administrative Science Quarterly, 17*(2), 178-184.

Clifford, M., & Marcus, G.E. (1986). *Writing culture: The poetics and politics of ethnography.* Berkeley, CA: University of California Press.

Cohen, M., & March, J. (1986). *Leadership and ambiguity: The American college president* (2nd ed.). Cambridge, MA: Harvard University Press.

Collison, M. (1988). Neglect of minorities seen jeopardizing future prosperity. *The Chronicle of Higher Education, XXXIV*(37), 1+.

Daly, R. (1990). Liminality and fiction in Cooper, Hawthorne, Cather, and Fitzgerald. In K. Ashley (Ed.), *Victor Turner and the construction of cultural criticism* (pp. 70-85). Bloomington, IN: Indiana University Press.

DeFlem, M. (1991). Ritual, anti-structure, and religion: A discussion of Victor Turner's processual symbolic analysis. *Journal for the Scientific Study of Religion. 30*(1), 1-25.

Douglas, M. (1982). *In the active voice.* Boston: Routledge and Kegan Paul.

Durkheim, E. (1915). *The elementary forms of the religious life: A study in religious sociology.* New York: Macmillan.

Eisner, E. (1979). *The educational imagination: On the design and evaluation of school programs.* New York: Macmillan.

Eisner, E. (1981). On the difference between scientific and artistic approaches to qualitative research. *Educational Researcher, 10*(4), 5-9.

Ellsworth, E. (1989). Why doesn't this feel empowering? Working through the repressive myths of critical pedagogy. *Harvard Educational Review, 59*(3), 297-324.

Ely, M. (1991). *Doing qualitative research: Circles within circles.* New York: Falmer Press.

Erlandson, D., Harris, E., Skipper, B., & Allen, S. (1993). *Doing naturalistic inquiry: A guide to methods.* Newbury Park, CA: Sage.

Fernandez, J.W. (1986a). *Persuasions and performances: The play of tropes in culture.* Bloomington, IN: Indiana University Press.

Fernandez, J.W. (1986b). The argument of images and the experience of returning to the whole. In V.W. Turner & E.M. Bruner (Eds.), *The anthropology of experience* (pp. 159-187). Urbana, IL: University of Illinois Press.

Flanigan, C.C. (1990). Liminality, carnival, and social structure. In K.M. Ashley (Ed.) *Victor Turner and the construction of cultural criticism* (pp. 42-63). Bloomington, IN: Indiana University Press.

Fleming, J. (1984). *Blacks in college.* San Francisco: Jossey-Bass.

Gardner, J. (1986, Summer). The freshman year experience. *College and University,* 261-274.

Gardner, J., & Van der Veer, G. (Eds.) (1998). *The senior year experience: Facilitating integration, reflection, closure, and transition.* San Francisco, CA: Jossey-Bass.

Garland, P. (1985). *Serving more than students: A critical need for college student personnel services.* ASHE-ERIC Higher Education Reports, (Serial No. 7). Washington, D.C.: ERIC Clearinghouse on Higher Education.

Geertz, C. (1973). *The interpretation of cultures.* New York: Basic Books.

Geertz, C. (1983). *Local knowledge.* New York: Basic Books.

Geertz, C. (1988). *Works and lives: The anthropologist as author.* Stanford, CA: Stanford University Press.

Giddens, A. (1979). *Central problems in social theory: Action, structure and contradiction in social analysis.* Berkeley, CA: University of California Press.

Giddens, A. (1982). *Profiles and critiques in social theory.* Berkeley, CA: University of California Press.

Giddens, A. (1984). *The constitution of society: Outline of the theory of structuralization.* Berkeley, CA: University of California Press.

Giddens, A. (1993). *New rules of sociological method: A positive critique of interpretative sociologies* (2nd ed.). Stanford, CA: Stanford University Press.

Gilligan, C. (1982). *In a different voice: Psychological theory and women's development.* Cambridge, MA: Harvard University Press.

Glaser, B. (1978). *Theoretical sensitivity.* San Francisco: University of California Press.

Glaser, B., & Strauss, A. (1965). Discovery of substantive theory: A basic strategy underlying qualitative research. *American Behavioral Scientist, 8,* 5-12.

Glaser, B., & Strauss, A. (1967). *The discovery of grounded theory.* Chicago: Aldine.

Goffman, E. (1959). *The presentation of self in everyday life.* Garden City, NY: Doubleday.

Goody, J. (1977). Against "ritual": Loosely structured thoughts on a loosely defined topic. In S. Moore & B. Myerhoff (Eds.), *Secular ritual* (pp. 25-35). Assen, Netherlands: Van Gorcum & Company.

Griffin, C. (1986). Qualitative methods and female experience: Young women from school to the job market In S. Wilkinson. (Ed.), *Feminist social psychology: Developing theory and practice* (pp. 173-191). Philadelphia: Open University Press.

Grimes, R.L. (1990). Victor Turner's definition, theory, and sense of ritual. In K. Ashley, (Ed.), *Victor Turner and the construction of cultural criticism: Between literature and anthropology* (pp. 141-146). Bloomington, IN: Indiana University Press.

Guba, E. (1978). *Toward a methodology of naturalistic inquiry in educational evaluation.* Los Angeles: Center for the Study of Evaluation.

Guba, E. (1985). The context of emergent paradigm research. In Y. Lincoln (Ed.), *Organizational theory and inquiry: The paradigm revolution* (pp. 79-104). Beverly Hills, CA: Sage.

Guba, E., & Lincoln, Y. (1982). Epistemelogical and methodological bases of naturalistic inquiry. *Educational Communications and Technical Journal. 30,* 233-252.

Guba, E., & Lincoln, Y. (1985). *Effective evaluation.* San Francisco: Jossey Bass.

Guba, E., & Lincoln, Y. (1986). The positivist and naturalist belief systems. Unpublished paper, Indiana University.

Guba, E., & Lincoln, Y. (1989). *Fourth generation evaluation.* Beverly Hills, CA: Sage.

Hawkins, B.C. (1989). Minority students on predominately white campuses: The need for a new commitment. *NASPA Journal, 26*(3), 175-179.

hooks, b. (1994). *Outlaw culture: Resisting representations.* New York: Routledge.

Kapferer, B. (1984). The ritual process and the problem of reflexivity in Sinhalese demon exorcisms. In J. MacAloon (Ed.), *Rite, drama, festival, spectacle: Rehearsals toward a theory of cultural performances* (pp. 179-207). Philadelphia: Institution for the Study of Human Issues.

Kapferer, B. (1986). Performance and the structuring of meaning and experience. In V.W. Turner & E.M. Bruner (Eds.). *The anthropology of experience* (pp. 188-203). Chicago: University of Illinois Press.

Katz, J. (1989). The challenge of diversity. In C. Woolbright (Ed.), *Valuing diversity on campus: A multicultural approach* (pp. 1-22). Bloomington, IN: Association of College Unions—International.

Kuh, G., Schuh, J., Whitt, E., & Associates (1991). *Involving colleges: Successful approaches to fostering student learning and development outside the classroom.* San Francisco: Jossey-Bass.

Kuh, G., & Whitt, E. (1988). *The invisible tapestry: Culture in American colleges and universities.* ASHE-ERIC- Higher Education Report, No. 1. Washington, D.C.: ERIC Clearinghouse on Higher Education.

Lather, P. (1991). *Getting smart: Feminist research and pedagogy with/in the postmodern.* New York: Routledge.

Lather, P. (1993). Fertile obsession: Validity after poststructuralism. *The Sociological Quarterly, 34*(4), 673-693.

Lederman, D. (1993, October 20). Old times not forgotten: A battle over symbols obscures University of Mississippi's racial charges. *The Chronicle of Higher Education,* A51-A52.

Leemon, T.A. (1972). *Rites of passage in a student culture.* New York: Teachers College Press.

Lenington, R.L. (1996). *Managing higher education as a business.* Phoenix, AZ: Oryx Press.

Levine, A. (July/August, 1997). Higher education becomes a mature industry. *About Campus,* 31-32.

Levi-Strauss, C. (1955). The structural study of myth. *Journal of American Folklore, 28,* 428-444.

Lewis, A. (1980). The ritual process and community development. *Community Development Journal, 15*(3), 190-199.

Lincoln, Y. (1985). The substance of the emergent paradigm: Implications for researchers. In Y. Lincoln (Ed.), *Organizational theory and inquiry: The paradigm revolution* (pp. 137-157). Beverly Hills, CA: Sage.

Lincoln, Y. (1995). Emerging criteria for quality in qualitative and interpretive research. *Qualitative Inquiry, 1*(3), 275-289.

Lincoln, Y., & Guba, E. (1985). *Naturalistic inquiry.* Beverly Hills, CA: Sage.

Lincoln, Y., & Guba, E. (1986). But is it rigorous? Trustworthiness and authenticity in naturalistic inquiry. In D. Williams (Ed.), *Naturalistic evaluation* (pp. 73-84). New Directions in Program Evaluation, 30. San Francisco: Jossey-Bass.

Lucas, C. (1985). Out at the edge: Notes on a paradigm shift. *Journal of Counseling and Development, 64,* 165-172.

MacAloon, J.J. (1984). Introduction: Cultural performances, culture theory. In J.J. MacAloon (Ed.), *Rite, drama, festival, spectacle: Rehearsals toward a theory of cultural performance* (pp. 1-15). Philadelphia: Institution for the Study of Human Issues.

Manning, K. (1989a). *Campus rituals and cultural meaning.* Unpublished doctoral dissertation. Bloomington, IN: Indiana University.

Manning, K. (1989b). Regalia, mortar boards, and meaning: The role of tradition in campus life. *Programming Magazine, 22*(3), 58-63.

Manning, K. (1993). Properties of institutional culture. In G. Kuh (Ed.), *Cultural perspectives in student affairs work* (pp. 21-36). Washington, D.C.: American College Personnel Association Media.

Manning, K. (1994a). Metaphorical analysis of a constructivist study of campus rituals. *Review of Higher Education, 18*(1), 45-60.

Manning, K. (1994b). Rituals and rescission: Building community in hard times. *Journal of College Student Development, 35*(4), 275-281.

Manning, K. (1997). Authenticity in constructivist inquiry: Methodological considerations without prescription. *Qualitative Inquiry, 3*(1), 93-115.

Manning, K., & Eaton, S. (1993). Loosening the ties that bind: Shaping student culture. In G. Kuh (Ed.), *Cultural perspectives in student affairs work* (pp. 95-109). Washington, D.C.: American College Personnel Association Media.

Marcus, G. (1988). Parody and the parodic in Polynesian cultural history. *Cultural Anthropology, 3*(1), 68-76.

McLaren, P. (1986). *Schooling as a ritual performance.* New York: Routledge and Kegan Paul.

Moore, S., & Myerhoff, B.G. (1977). Secular ritual: Forms and meaning. In S. Moore & B.G. Myerhoff (Eds.). *Secular ritual* (pp. 3-24). Assen, Netherlands: van Gorcum.

Morgan, S. (1984). Borges's "Immortal": Metaritual, metaliterature, metaperformance. In J.J. MacAloon (Ed.), *Rite, drama, festival, spectacle: Rehearsals toward a theory of cultural performance* (pp. 79-101). Philadelphia: Institution for the Study of Human Issues.

Myerhoff, B. (1977). We don't wrap herring in a printed page: Fusion, fictions and continuity in secular ritual. In S. Moore & B. Myerhoff (Eds.), *Secular ritual* (pp. 199-224). Assen, Netherlands: van Gorcum.

Myerhoff, B. (1978). *Number our days: A triumph of continuity and culture among Jewish old people in an urban ghetto.* New York: Simon and Schuster.

Myerhoff, B. (1984). A death in due time: Construction of self and culture in ritual drama. In J. MacAloon (Ed.), *Rite, drama, festival, spectacle: Rehearsals toward a theory of cultural performances* (pp. 149-178). Philadelphia: Institution for the Study of Human Issues.

Oosten, J. (1993). Examining the theoretical discourse on ritual. *Current Anthropology, 34*(1), 106-108.

Oring, E. (1993). Victor Turner, Sigmund Freud, and the return of the repressed. *Ethos, 21*(3), 273-294.

Orphanides, A.G. (1992). An overview of theories on symbolism and interpretation. *Journal of Business and Society, 5*, 103-111.

Ortner, S. B. (1984).Theory in anthropology since the sixties. *Comparative Studies in Society and History, 2*(6), 126-166.

Pascarella, E.T., & Terenzini, P.T. (1991). *How college affects students: Findings and insights from twenty years of research.* San Francisco: Jossey-Bass.

Patton, M. (1990). *Qualitative evaluation methods.* Beverly Hills, CA: Sage.

Perry, W. (1970). *Forms of intellectual and ethical development in the college years: A scheme.* Troy, MO: Holt, Rinehart & Winston.

Polanyi, M. (1983). *The tacit dimension.* Gloucester, MA: Peter Smith.

Popper, K. (1959). Prediction and prophecy in social sciences. In P. Gardiner (Ed.), *Theories of history* (pp. 275-285). Chicago: The Free Press.

Powdermaker, H. (1966). *Stranger and friend: The way of an anthropologist.* New York: W.W. Norton & Company.

Rabinow, P. (1977). *Reflections of fieldwork in Morocco.* Berkeley, CA: University of California Press.

Rappaport, R.A. (1992). Ritual, time, and eternity. *Zygon, 27*(1), 5-30.

Raybin, D. (1990). Aesthetics, romance, and Turner. In K. Ashley (Ed.), *Victor Turner and the construction of cultural criticism* (pp. 21-41). Bloomington, IN: Indiana University Press.

Sanday, P.R. (1979). The ethnographic paradigm. *Anthropological Studies Quarterly, 24*, 527-538.

Schaef, A.W. (1985). *Women's reality: An emerging female system in a white male society.* Minneapolis, MN: Winston Press.

Schwartzman, J. (1982). Symptoms and rituals: Paradoxical modes and social organization. *Ethos, 10*(1), 3-25.

Shea, C. (1993, November 10). A cloud over symbols: Once-honored college mascots like Indians and Minuteman now irk many on nation's campuses. *The Chronicle of Higher Education*, p. A33, A35.

Singer, M. (1984). *Man's glassy essence: Explorations in semiotic anthropology.* Bloomington, IN: Indiana University Press.

Skrtic, T. (1985). Doing naturalistic research in educational organizations. In Y. Lincoln (Ed.), *Organizational theory and inquiry: The paradigm revolution* (pp. 185-200). Beverly Hills, CA: Sage.

Smircich, L. (1986). Behind the debate over the validity of alternative paradigm research. Unpublished paper. University of Massachusetts at Amherst.

Smith, J.K. (1983). Quantitative versus qualitative research: An attempt to clarify the issue. *Educational Researcher. 15*, 4-12.

Smith, J.K. & Hershusius, L. (1986). Closing down the conversation: The end of the quantitative-qualitative debate among educational inquirers. *Educational Researcher, 15*, 4-12.

Smith, J.K. (1990). Alternative research paradigms and the problem of criteria. In E.G. Guba (Ed.), *The paradigm dialog* (pp. 167-187). Newbury Park, CA: Sage.

Spindler, G.D. (1987). *Education and cultural process: Anthropological approaches* (2nd ed.). Prospect Heights, IL: Waveland Press.

Stage, F.K., & Manning, K. (1992). *Enhancing the multicultural environment. A cultural brokering approach.* New Directions in Student Services Series, 60. San Francisco: Jossey-Bass.

Strauss, A., & Corbin, J. (1990). *Basics of qualitative research: Grounded theory procedures and techniques.* Newbury Park, CA: Sage.

Sturrock, J. (Ed.). (1979). *Structuralism: From Levi-Strauss to Derrida.* New York: Oxford University Press.

Tierney, W.G. (1988). Organizational culture in higher education. *Journal of Higher Education, 59*(1), 1-21.

Turner, F. (1990). "Hyperion to a satyr": Criticism and anti-structure in the work of Victor Turner. In K. Ashley (Ed.). *Victor Turner and the construction of cultural criticism: Between literature and anthropology* (pp. 147-162). Bloomington, IN: Indiana University Press.

Turner, T. (1977). Transformation, hierarchy and transcendence: A reformulation of van Gennep's model of the structure of rites of passage. In S. Moore & B. Myerhoff (Eds.), *Secular ritual* (pp. 53-70). Assen, Netherlands: van Gorcum.

Turner, V. (1967). Betwixt and between: The liminal period in *Rites of Passage*. In V. Turner (Ed.), *The Forest of Symbols* (pp. 93-111). Ithaca, NY: Cornell University Press.

Turner, V. (1969). *The ritual process: Structure and anti-structure.* Chicago: Aldine.

Turner, V. (1972). Comments and conclusions. In B.A. Babcock (Ed.), *The reversible world* (pp. 276-296). Ithaca, NY: Cornell University Press.

Turner, V. (1974). *Dramas, fields, and metaphors: Symbolic action in human society.* Ithaca, NY: Cornell University Press.

Turner, V. (1977a). Symbols in African ritual. In J. Dolgin, D. Kemnitzer, & D. Schneider (Eds.). *Symbolic anthropology: A reader in the study of symbols and meanings* (pp. 183-194). New York: Columbia University Press.

Turner, V. (1977b). Variations and a theme of liminality. In S. Moore & B. Myerhoff (Eds.), *Secular ritual* (pp. 36-52). Assen, Netherlands: van Gorcum.

Turner, V. (1984). Liminality and the performative genres. In J.J. MacAloon (Ed.), *Rite, drama, festival, spectacle: Rehearsals toward a theory of cultural performance* (pp. 19-41). Philadelphia: Institution for the Study of Human Issues.

Turner, V., & Turner, E. (Eds.) (1985). *On the edge of the bush: Anthropology as experience*. Tucson, AZ: University of Arizona Press.

Van Gennep, A. (1960). *The rites of passage*. Chicago: University of Chicago Press.

Van Maanen, J. (1979). Reclaiming qualitative methods for organizational research: A preface. *Administrative Science Quarterly, 24*(4), 520-526.

Weick, K. (1979). *The social psychology of organizing* (2nd ed.). Reading, MA: Addison-Wesley.

Wolcott, H. (1984). Ethnographers sans ethnography: The evaluation compromise. In D.M. Fetterman (Ed.), *Ethnography in educational evaluation* (pp. 177-210). Beverly Hills, CA: Sage.

Index

About the Author

KATHLEEN MANNING is Associate Professor of Higher Education and Student Affairs Administration at the University of Vermont.

ISBN 0-89789-504-5

90000>

EAN

9 780897 895040

HARDCOVER BAR CODE